VIRTUAL SPACES

SEX AND THE CYBER CITIZEN

VIRTUAL SPACES

SEX AND THE CYBER CITIZEN

Cleo Odzer, Ph.D.

B
BERKLEY BOOKS, NEW YORK

This book is an original publication of The Berkley Publishing Group.

VIRTUAL SPACES

A Berkley Book / published by arrangement with
the author

PRINTING HISTORY
Berkley trade paperback edition / November 1997

The Putnam Berkley World Wide Web site address is
http://www.berkley.com

ISBN: 0-425-15986-8

BERKLEY®
Berkley Books are published by The Berkley Publishing Group,
a member of Penguin Putnam Inc.,
200 Madison Avenue, New York, New York 10016.
BERKLEY and the ''B'' design are trademarks belonging to Berkley
Publishing Corporation.

PRINTED IN THE UNITED STATES OF AMERICA

10 9 8 7 6 5 4 3 2 1

Contents

VIRTUAL SPACES

SEX AND THE CYBER CITIZEN

Introduction

I followed him to his home, but we didn't enter the house. He stopped at the patio entrance and said, "Here we are." I looked around. The garden had bushes tall enough to ensure privacy from passersby. A blackbird flew by. He came close and touched my cheek: "You scared, my pet?"

I knew his reputation for violence, but I'd also seen him enough times to be totally aroused by his presence. Being alone with him had me on fire. I giggled. "A little."

"You should be," he answered as he brought his face close to mine and kissed my nose.

Suddenly he grabbed my shoulders and flung me around, tying my arms behind me. He dragged me over to a tree and looped the rope to a hook on a branch. He stood back and watched as I dangled helplessly. Evening was approaching, forming long shadows along the grass and patio tiles. No one was in sight though an occasional sound could be heard from the house.

He stepped close and ran his hands roughly over my breasts. "Are you wet, my pet?" he asked as he inserted one of his legs between mine, forcing them apart.

"Yes. You make me hot."

He smiled and ran his hand under my skirt and brusquely moved aside the crotch of my panties to rub his finger over my cunt lips.

I moaned.

He jammed two fingers deeply inside me, a sharp plunging invasion of my innermost person. I groaned and moved my hips as his fingers plunged in and out. "Yes, yes," I said breathlessly, "that feels so good. Finger me."

I leaned my head forward, wanting to rest it against him, wanting urgently to touch him, but he pulled back and took his hands off me.

"You want me to fuck you, don't you?"

"Yes, please, I'm burning for you."

With a riding crop he lashed at my breasts, tearing the fabric of my blouse and said, "Where? Where do you want it?"

I flinched at the pain and felt my groin surge with heat. He struck again, this time aiming his blow across my right nipple. I cried out and whispered, "Everywhere. I want you in my mouth, my cunt, my ass. Fuck me. I ache for you."

He unzipped his trousers and his erect penis made my breath come in short pants. I couldn't take my eyes off it. "Yes, yes," I moaned. "I want it in me. Let me suck it. I want your cock in my mouth, filling it, owning it."

He unhooked me from the tree and ordered, "Get on your knees."

I fell to my knees, eyes slitted in passion. He raised his hand and brought the crop smacking down on my ass as he grabbed my hair and pulled my face to his crotch. I opened my mouth, waiting hungrily to feel his penis pass over my lips—

The cursor on my computer froze.

"OH SHIT!" I wailed at the screen. "NOOOOOOO! Now is not the time for a crash."

I tried to cancel out, I tried to restart the computer, I clicked furiously on the track ball—all to no avail. I'd crashed; one of those mysterious freezes that happen all too often.

His last statement, that he stood with his cock poised before my face, lingered there on the screen, dead. I could get no closer to him and he had probably received the message that I'd disconnected.

"SHIT!" I said aloud once more before resigning myself to the fact that I had to shut off the whole control panel, even momentarily plunging my desk area into darkness as the lights also went out. I hoped he wouldn't log off, thinking I'd deserted him.

As erotic as what you just read was, it was only on paper, and a dim evocation of the real thing—the real virtual thing, that is. A good cyber-sex encounter is totally absorbing. Your mind and body are completely focused on your virtual reality. You're plugged right into the fantasy part of your brain, but now someone else is interacting with it. The vagaries of real life—a doorbell, a news story breaking on CNN, a real-life party going on elsewhere— cannot compete with the compelling nature of this phenomenon. It's all-consuming. Your brain is alive and engaged with another cyber citizen, one equally committed to the cyber way of life. We who live there—cyber citizens—live in the virtual reality (VR) world. We participate in real life (RL), too, of course. But our First World exists in the computer. The political economists of the nineteenth century would laugh if they knew what we've done to their term *First World*. To us it no longer represents Capitalism. It's the main world to which we belong, the cyber world. Cyber citizenship exists; I know it because I live it. My home is in cyberspace.

This new world mirrors the old in various ways. The passions, jealousies, obsessions, needs are no less strong than their real-life counterparts because they trigger the same internal emotional states. A cybersex scene can be as arousing as a real one. There is no physical touch among lovers and no pain in cyber masochism; yet cyber love affairs call out feelings no less intense than real ones.

Cyber sex is identical to real sex in many ways and is different in others. The love, passions, and torment that emerge from cyber relationships depend on dynamics that develop in RL but that manifest themselves more explicitly in cyberspace. So subtle are these dynamics in real life that people aren't even aware of them. It is on the net that our innermost secrets are revealed in all their agonizing beauty.

Part of all relationships exists only in our minds, and this is what is undeniable in cyber passion—when we don't know what our love object looks like, have never heard his or her voice, can't be sure of age or even gender, then we realize that the emotions come from within our-

> A new dimension of human experience is rapidly opening up. . . . However, the experience created by computers and computer networks can in many ways be understood as a psychological "space." When they power up their computers, launch a program, write email, or log on to their online service, users often feel—consciously or subconsciously—that they are entering a "place" or "space" that is filled with a wide array of meanings and purposes. Many users who have telneted to a remote computer or explored the World Wide Web will describe the experience as "traveling" or "going someplace." Spatial metaphors—such as "worlds," "domains," or "rooms" are common in articulating online activities. On an even more basic psychological level, users often describe how their computer is an extension of their mind and personality, a "space" that reflects their tastes, attitudes, and interests. In psychoanalytic terms, computers and cyberspace become a type of "transitional space" that is an extension of the individual's intrapsychic world. (Suler, May 1996)

selves. The passion that arises from net sex exists within us.

We can learn much about the psychology of our species from this new world. Beyond that, it is fun, it is engaging, it is pleasurable.

Welcome to the sex world of the new millennium.

Cyberspace brings you face-to-face with who you are at your root (or "/root" as we say in computer lingo). All social interaction combines our inner and outer worlds, but cyberspace provides an especially versatile medium for externalizing the internal.

While some virtual spaces are down-to-earth realms, others lean toward fantasia. In places like MOOs [*M*UD (Multi-User Domain) *O*bject *O*riented] and on the Palace (a type of graphical MOO with sound), you can create an imaginary world and write programs to make your fantasy objects do whatever you want. Then other people interact with your inventions, bringing them to life. It allows people to script a world, live in it, and bring others to live in it, too; the VR and RL emotional realms run parallel. I've dredged up my wildest dreams and set them in motion, but I didn't realize until later that I was externalizing my psyche and showing people my innermost desires and distresses.

I once needed to speak to an online woman about planning an event. When my requests for a private conversation went unanswered, I sensed a dismissal of my existence, possibly a historic feeling stemming from early interactions with my mother. Though I later learned the woman had just started a paying online job and was too flustered with new responsibilities to attend to acquaintances, I nevertheless ripped into her. When she greeted my cyber arrival with, *Hi, girlfriend!* I answered, *Cut the hypocrisy, bitch. I'll take no more bullshit from you.*

Whoa—the anger I dredged up and flung through the modem was a shocking discovery.

The motivation for cyber actions comes from within each individual cybernaut. Whether posing as a TV star or as a rodent, beneath it all we are ourselves. Often when

> We have an inner life that while having constant exchanges with the outer environment, has an enduring life of its own. It becomes the essence of the individual. Its organization is what we call the "inner self." (Arieti, 1974)

online, I experience a frightening flash of insight. I catch a glimpse of my inner demons and feel their power. Yikes, what is this lust I feel? What is this longing, this torment? There haven't been many times when I've exhibited embarrassing out-of-control behaviors, but cyberspace has roused me to that point. Once, my cyber boyfriend Jagwire had misdirected a private message meant for a female friend and had sent it to me by mistake. In fury, I shut off the modem and insulted him in email for a week. After looking back at the things I'd said and cringing in shame, we made up. I apologized and confessed to being so overwhelmed by passion that I'd behaved like an idiot. In truth, I didn't know if Jagwire had six heads and a beer belly. With his home in California and mine in New York, we'd never met in RL. Nevertheless, I'd been totally captivated, and when I suspected unfaithfulness, I was crushed. Neither my substantial past love affairs nor my scholastic degrees had affected my romantic idealization of this person I knew only as a name on a computer screen.

Raw unalloyed emotion—that was my reaction to an imagined affront. I couldn't avoid the fact that what had sparked the outburst existed only in my mind. Jealousy resided in me, ready to be awakened by the firing of a neurotransmitter associated with who-knew-what memory. Perhaps I had reconnected to an old feeling of rejection from my mother. Perhaps an old nerve had been hit that said, "You don't care about my feelings." Perhaps his mispage had made me feel that I was too worthless for him to be careful where he sent his messages. My emotional reaction had little to do with him—it came from the previous events in my life that made me "me." My behavior in the virtual relationship followed patterns I'd established in RL relationships, some imprinted back in childhood.

Frequently, online interactions hit a nerve that makes me behave in irrational ways. I have to recognize the reaction as something within me, especially since the person who "caused" the reaction is someone I've never met, whose voice I've never heard, and whose age or sex I can't verify. I've spent so much time in cyberspace, I see the world through the eyes of a CPU (a computer's Central Processing Unit), and I've grown to appreciate that CPU eyes can be a window into one's soul. I've looked deeply at myself through these eyes and have descended to the core of the database that is me. Sometimes, when I've been hurt by something a stranger did online, I've found that the original blueprint of the scene was created with my mother decades ago, now replayed in an updated cyberspace version. When an online character who is supposed to care about me acts in a way that seems unmindful, it triggers the response of feeling "invisible," how I always felt around my mother.

During adolescence, we awaken sexually. Sexuality is a basic motivator, as strong as the need for food and sleep. It should surprise no one that sexuality is a major force behind online communications. It comes out, often unexpectedly, because we are sexual beings. We become attracted to a name on the screen regardless of the fact that we've never met the person in the flesh. A romantic episode happens early in a traveler's foray into cyberspace. With love comes sex, and then an easy slip into anonymous cyber slutting. Net sex seems so safe. After all, it's not real.

And, as with everything else, sexuality is expressed through our historic selves. What attracts me to someone? What little comment does someone utter that tweaks my body's arousal? It happens, and often.

It's my nature to take things to the extreme, and I've grown accustomed to living on the edge. I've been to the outer limits so often it seems like my normal state. I look around and see unknown territory and I think: Here I am again, out on a limb.

Traveling into cyberspace has taken me to that distant realm. I've journeyed into the abyss, looking back at the great distance to the desk chair in front of the Macintosh. The science-fiction films that show a person swallowed into the screen, out of real space and into cyberspace, have the right idea, but the wrong image. The physical body doesn't go through the modem. But part of your being does float out the phone line into another universe, and it's not science fiction. Cyber life is real. It's a place in your mind where you're joined to the minds of others.

Although cyberspace is called virtual reality, this book will show that it's not so different from real life. Virtual spaces provide real communities, and through this new perspective, we can examine human behavior from another angle. After living for seven years in the online world, I've pledged allegiance to citizenship of this new culture.

Our real-world self always interacts with our cyber self, so transformations are individualistic and actual. The cyber world is just another arena in which to express ourselves. If I'm in an online gaming situation, such as a MUD (Multi-User Domain), try as I might to act like a cockroach, my personal quirks will show through. If I have a hang-up about physical distance and I'm approached by another cyber roach whose antennae are too close to mine, I will react as me not as a roach: *Hey buddy, get your antenna outta my face.*

Long before the advent of the cyber world, renowned psychologist and personality theorist Carson (1969:25-26), discussing the interpersonal nature of personality, explained how we are formed in our relationship to others.

According to Sullivan, "personality is the relatively enduring pattern of recurrent interpersonal situations which characterize a human life" (1953:110-11). . . . It should be noted that an "interpersonal situation," as Sullivan uses the term, requires the participation of only one "real" person, in that any other "persons" in any particular instance may be wholly illusory—that is, products of the real person's imaginations or fantasies. . . . Strictly speaking, then, personality is nothing more (or less) than the patterned regularities that may be observed in an individual's relations with other persons, who may be real in the sense of actually being present, real but absent and hence "personified," or illusory.

Sexuality is also a personal thing. Many of our wants, desires, and kinks stem from early experiences. When it comes to cyber sex, a whole other arena opens up. We can act out the sexual fantasies we'd never consider doing in RL, the fantasies we wouldn't want to do in RL. We can switch gender and switch gender preferences. Everything is possible, and this book will show that the Internet generation is, in fact, trying out these sexual possibilities, ranging from hard-core net addicts who never engage in cyber sex to hard-core cyber-sex addicts who've had to cancel their net accounts because cyber sex was overriding everything else in their lives.

I will trace my development as an online sexual persona, starting on CompuServe in 1990; finding Echo, a New York City bbs (Bulletin Board System) in 1991; expanding to the Internet, the Web, the MOOs in 1994; the Palace in 1995; and on to CUseeme in 1996. I will also recount the experiences of other cyber citizens in their travels into this new world. Hopefully my journey, and those of others, will inspire your own cyber wanderings.

1. Hot Chat

In cyberspace, without physical or even visual contact, people still fall passionately in love. Unfortunately, since the computer brings together people from all over the world, the couple is usually not on the same continent. Eventually some do meet in person and some get married in RL. There are many VR weddings.

It is not my intention to discredit online romances as out of touch with reality. On the contrary, I aim to show that the experience is a reality. VR is as real as RL.

My first cyber infatuation was with a man named Fire on CompuServe in 1990. I'd become addicted to CompuServe's CB simulator, where you communicated directly with people, modeled after CB radio. CompuServe's CB was a "chat" space. All forms of text-based chat share the same format:

> . . . a dynamic form of communication: new comments appear at the bottom of your screen as you watch, and older comments scroll off the top of your screen. Somewhere in the world, a human being has typed those words on a keyboard, no

more than a couple seconds ago; if you know the right words to say in response, you can leap into the conversation and make that person and others around the world laugh out loud, grow angry, feel lustful. (Rheingold)

Our initial set of questions: "What first attracted you? What got you interested? What fascinated you most?" elicited detailed accounts of attraction online. Participants reported a variety of reasons for their initial attraction in response to these questions. Many people identified senders as attractive when they were able to identify things in common with the sender of the message: similar values, ideas and interests. Humor was mentioned by many respondents as one quality which attracted them to their particular mate.

For those mainly interested in a sexual encounter, similar sexual preferences or desires were a first indicator of initial attraction, as well as other qualities such as a wry wit. Interviewees tried to gauge physical attractiveness of the online lover using other factors, such as the person's self-description in personal ads, bios, or during the course of conversation online. Since people were not in the physical presence of the other person, but rather were dealing with the "simulated self," a hyperreality presented by the other person, the people we interviewed sometimes seemed to only tentatively accept the simulation as "real." (Albright:9)

CB had hundreds of specialized "channels," such as a channel for teens, one for gays, another for senior citizens, and even one for sadomasochists. CB channels, in those days, generally held ten to thirty people (now they go over one hundred). Some people wrote publicly for everyone on the channel; some sent private messages to individuals. On CB, we used "handles" instead of names. My handle was "Goa," named after the hippie beach in India where I spent six years. I'd been on CB less than a week when Fire sent a private message: *Fire says hello*. After a hello back, he suggested we go into a one-on-one group so we wouldn't have to keep sending private messages. Fire told me he was a physicist. I told him I had just received my doctorate degree.

Since I was new to the online chat world, some of the awe I felt for the medium probably associated itself with Fire. I was hooked on chat and on Fire. The next day I looked for him. Again he invited me into a private session. *I found your dissertation*, he said.

Where? I asked, surprised.

I did an IQuest search here on CI$ and it turned up the abstract. Plus the name of everyone on your dissertation committee. (CompuServe is abbreviated to CIS, but we users call it CI$ because it charges extra money for everything.)

Really? Wow! I had no idea that dissertations were listed anywhere. To find my work accessible to the world delighted me no end. I was especially thrilled that Fire had taken the time to look me up.

I fell in cyber love. My whole day centered around when I'd be in chat with Fire.

I knew he had a wife, but that didn't prevent my excitement at seeing him listed online, or my disappointed when I rushed home from work to log on but found him absent. At that time my defenses against RL married men hadn't carried over into cyberspace. I hadn't yet learned that the "virtual" in VR didn't mean it wasn't real. One night I found Fire online, but after we exchanged a few private messages, he didn't ask me to join him in a group. Crushed to the bone is what I felt.

I waited half an hour after our banter in private messages ran out, and then when there were no more communications from him, I logged off, depressed.

An interesting attraction of CB was "hot chat." My first experience with hot chat happened on another area of CompuServe—the Human Sexuality forum. I'd heard about it from a friend who'd sent me a modem as a present, and my curiosity had been tweaked. It was CompuServe that originally introduced me to online communications. The first time on CI$, I ventured into HSX, as the Human Sexuality forum was called. Within minutes I felt a surge of panic. In addition to hot chat, CompuServe also gave me my first experience with Menu Hell, a place I'm now familiar with but that totally frazzled me that day. For a decade I'd been a computer geek and had taught BASIC programming as a college undergraduate. When I hid out on a remote island in Thailand for seven months to write my dissertation, I typed it into a laptop while lazing under a palm tree. So I was no stranger to the frustrations of the computer-related learning curve. But CI$'s menu maze freaked me out, as I was also being deluged with private *Hello!*s and had no idea how to respond.

There must have been a gang of men waiting for a female name to log into HSX. I was trapped in menus, trying to find the chat area and *Hello, what are u wearing?* and *Hello, what are you in the mood for?* and *Hello, how old are you?* popped up urgently, expecting an answer. I saw only options one, two, three, four, five, none of which took me anywhere except to another set of options. Comparable to Menu Hell is the Web's Link List Hell. I follow a link on a list only to find another list of links leading to another list. Same aggravation.

Finally, finally, I got to the "conference" area on HSX and could chat. In no time I joined some man in a private group and engaged in my first hot chat. My partner knew it was my virgin ride and was sweet and attentive. I found it fascinating and erotic and oh so interesting, though not particularly memorable. It was purely an anonymous sex act. My sole intent had been to try it out.

After a few nights of disappointment when I didn't see Fire online or I saw him but didn't get encouraging flirtations, we found ourselves finally in a private group, and the conversation turned to sex. I knew how computer sex worked from my foray into HSX. By this time I was gung-ho to hold Fire in my cyber arms. We slipped easily into a sexual tryst that plunged me into a cyber relationship. I was in love.

On CB, two people form a private group with the commands *invite* and *join,* and they type each other into orgasms. One of my sexual interludes in a private group with Fire went like this:

Fire: can i kiss your clitoris?
Goa: i'd love it

Fire: smooooooooooooch

Goa: mmm

Fire: punctuated with a tongue-fleck

Goa: wonderful

Fire: what do your tits look like?

Goa: I'm plugging in my vibrator

Goa: firm

Fire: how big?

Goa: 34B, my left one has a beauty mark on the nipple

Fire: mmmm perfect size—would love to take a nipple between my lips & suck it

Goa: I'm imagining you doing that

Fire: i love eating pussy

Goa: mmmmm, do it

Goa: are you hard?

Fire: i love getting pussy juice all over my face

Fire: yes i'm hard & little clear droplets are forming at the tip of my cock

Goa: my pussy is getting juicy

Fire: I'm burying my face in your pussy & sucking licking & tonguing

Goa: hmm I love it. I want to touch your cock

Fire: mmm sit on it, envelop it

Goa: I want it in me, deep

Fire: mmmmmmm yes deep

Goa: ooooooooo

Fire: aaaaaaaaaaaa

Fire: ooops gotta go

Goa: i'm rubbing . . . Huh?

Fire: shit somebody at the door

Goa: WHAT!

Fire leaves the group

Unfortunately, Fire had a habit of disappearing quickly when his wife returned from her aerobics class. I'm sure that turning off his computer without shutting it down properly was as harmful to the computer as it was to my ego. CompuServe's CB was overrun with married men seeking electronic adultery.

At first, I found hot chat a nifty novelty but soon grew bored. The verbal format repeated itself like a trashy novel. When ardor grew, words contracted to long ahhhhhhs, or oooohs, or ummmmmms. While one hand masturbated, the other—usually the less dexterous—typed. When I found myself faking orgasms in order to log off gracefully, I decided hot chat had lost its appeal.

Fire's sudden disappearances really annoyed me, too. He'd left me in the lurch more than once, and eventually we had a fight and the relationship ended. I was in a dark mood for days. Those hours every night, either in a private group with Fire or on a channel waiting to see if Fire turned up, sent my CI$ bill skyrocketing to over a hundred dollars a month. Fortunately, that was when I joined Echo, a bbs (Bulletin Board System). By that time I'd had enough of hot chat and restless married men. I wanted a live human.

Although I had RL love affairs over the next six years, the VR ones continued, off and on, and no less passionately.

We cyber citizens have different way of incorporating our computer sexuality into our lives. Suzy, an Echo friend of mine, also began her cyber life on CompuServe, or rather the Source, what CompuServe was called before it was named CompuServe. Suzy, too, found hot chat exciting at first. "This person was writing these special words just for me. It was very arousing." She was so aroused that she soon found herself doing the "one-handed typing" thing, typing long oooooohs and ahhhhhhhhs while masturbating. She laughed recalling that "I was just about to have an orgasm, when I fell off the stool and ended up with the keyboard on my chest."

Nevertheless, hot chat, though stimulating at the beginning, soon lost its zip, and Suzy progressed the way of many CB'ers—she graduated to phone sex. On the rare occasion that I visit CB nowadays, it's not long after entering a private group with someone that he'll suggest a phone call. The guys will call you no matter how far away you live or how long the call will take.

Suzy moved from chatting with men online, to having phone sex with them, to meeting the occasional one in person. None of these turned into RL romances—though some did end in an RL sexual fling, just to satisfy the hunger built up from the long phone/computer affair. Usually, though, the illusion ended as soon as Suzy met her computer mate in person. The men were thrilled to meet her, petite and beautiful as she is, but she was often disappointed to find her VR beau was an RL beast.

Phone sex never interested me for several reasons. First, I didn't want someone tape-recording my voice. I've saved screen captures of cyber-sex encounters that were particularly delicious and I imagine that guys do the same, with text and with phone conversations. These can be

> A great many of our respondents seemed to follow a similar trajectory for their online relationships. Once having met online, they soon exchange phone numbers and call each other, often exchange photos, followed by what we have termed a fleshmeet (the time when the two online lovers first meet in person). We were interested in this trajectory, and in how and when people decide to take these various steps in moving the relationship from online to offline. Many interviewees reported an escalation in the number of phone calls and email or time spent online chatting, as the attraction between the online lovers grew. (Albright: 11)

read or replayed at a later date and enjoyed anew. I didn't want my conversations recorded for the same reason I never posed nude during my modeling days: I didn't want my voice in a sex call turning up somewhere in the future. After living six years on a hippie beach in Goa where people were nude most of the time, I'm sure there are plenty of nude shots of me somewhere. I've even shown videos of myself on that beach on public-access TV. Still, naked on a nude beach feels different than posing naked for a picture, and the thought of someone having my voice in a taped sex conversation is a turnoff.

Second, I didn't want the person calling me again. It's one thing to have a spontaneous fling. It's another to have some strange man in possession of your phone number. So I never got involved in that the way Suzy did.

Eight years later Suzy still has the occasional cyber-turned-phone-sex affair, though she now knows it's not Prince Charming on the other end of the line. Suzy, however, never experienced the other areas of the net where I found the cyber sex to be compelling, satisfying, and addicting.

To me hot chat is the lowest form of cyber sex. The higher levels involve greater technology and more computer expertise. Hot chat is rampant on other low-end environments, such as IRC (Internet Relay Chat) and in "Talk." In Talk, the computer screen is split in two and one person types in the top half, the other in the bottom. Janet met her boyfriend in person, but, unfortunately, he lives in England and she lives in New York. Their love affair has continued for three years now, with one or two in-person meetings a year, plus daily hot-chat sessions via Talk. Janet finds their Talk-sex sufficient to continue their intimacy while they are physically apart.

Cyber citizens move in various ways along their cyber-affair paths. Cyber sex exists in different levels of computer sophistication, plus some cyber citizens have RL reunions while some couples never meet in person, though the affair continues for years.

My own cyber trajectory first took me from hot chat on CompuServe to an RL romance on Echo.

Eleven of us newusers sat in a Greenwich Village apartment when he walked in, a thin man with brown hair, blue eyes, and glasses. Grouped around the computer that embodied Echo, we turned to see the latest arrival. Though I'd figured out the basics of the system, I went to Echo school to learn the details and to meet some of the people I'd communicated with electronically. We newusers may have exchanged greetings online, but this was our first f2f (face-to-face) encounter, and every arrival brought a curious, "Who are you?"

"I'm Jeremy Berg," the guy at the door answered.

The people closest to him introduced themselves as the rest turned back to listen to Stacy Horn, the owner of Echo, who instructed us on how to use the system. Tiny, with brown bangs and pixie hair, Stacy's cuteness and fragility belied the competent thirty-six-year-old woman she was. I caught only a snatch of her sentence as I swiveled for another look at Jeremy Berg to reassess the thought he aroused in me: I'm in love.

Jeremy caught my eye, and I mouthed, "I'm Cleo."

Jeremy and I had written messages to each other in the two weeks since I'd joined Echo. We users described ourselves in our "bio" files so other Echoids (as we called ourselves) could find out something about us. Jeremy had read my bio—anthropologist, elephant tattoo on my foot—and knew of my blond hair and blue eyes. He nodded and pantomimed that I looked like he'd imagined. I'd never pictured him at all. My impression from his messages was that he was an asshole. Now, seeing him in person, I was captivated.

Echo was composed of "conferences" on topics such

as politics, sex, culture, psychology. You could write a comment in an item at one P.M. and someone might answer two hours later. If you logged on to Echo once a day, you'd find responses to the things you wrote the day before.

A special feature of Echo was the "yo." Yo's enabled you to communicate directly with whoever was online at the time. Being a local New York City bbs, Echo constituted a friendly community, and old-timers generally yo-ed newusers.

During my first ten minutes on Echo, my computer beeped three times and a message flashed on screen:

[. . . Yo!!!!!!! this message comes from drliz (Liz Margoshes).

Hi, Cleo. Welcome to Echo.]

Stacy had given Liz the login name "drliz" because Echo had several Lizes and this one had a Ph.D. Echo's membership included many degreed women, which pleased me.

Jeremy had also yo-ed me that day and many times since. He'd yo-ed me too often. I sensed a desperation in him to converse with a female. Male attention flattered me, but overacknowledgment from one who'd never met me lost its impact as a compliment. I'd labeled him "loser."

Echo also had a space to chat, though it wasn't used much. Echoids communicated mostly through yo's and through responses in conferences and they didn't engage in anonymous hot chat. Not only could you not be anonymous on Echo, the local bbs had real parties and get-togethers, so most people knew each other in RL. For the past month I'd been getting close to Brent, a man I'd met at a Mensa dinner. After Fire, it was nice to be attracted to a live person for a change, with whom I might have real body-to-body contact. After meeting Brent at the weekly Mensa get-together, I'd returned every Friday night to sit next to him. When I joined Echo and realized its wonderment, I pressed Brent to join, too. On Echo, we spent hours a night yo-ing each other or speaking directly in chat.

Often, when Brent and I entered chat to have a conversation, Jeremy barged in. Echo's chat displayed names for who said what and alerted you when someone entered or left. It also had a way to send private messages, and Brent and I would send each other disparaging remarks about the intruder along with cutesy stuff, analogous to playing footsie under a table. Parentheses signaled private messages.

One time in chat:

Brent: I logged on to Echo from the office again today

Cleo: Shame on you. Stealing time again, huh?

Brent: I have to wait for lunch when people leave the room

Cleo: My office computer died today because it was full of cat hair

Jeremy [login]

Cleo: hi, Jeremy

Brent: hello, Jeremy

(private message from Brent): here he is again

(send Brent) groan

Jeremy: hello, y'all. What's up?

Cleo: cat hair in my office computer

Jeremy: what kind of work do you do Cleo?

Cleo: statistical analysis in a drug rehab.

(private message from Brent): doesn't he realize it's always just the two of us in here?

(send Brent) he doesn't seem to care

Jeremy: where's your office?

(send Brent) pinch

(private message from Brent): ouch!

Cleo: I'd prefer jungle fieldwork but I work at 40th between 5th and 6th

(private message from Brent): tickle tickle

(send Brent) giggle. Tickle back

Jeremy: where do you live?

Cleo: mid-Manhattan, 50 seconds from the office

(private message from Brent): why don't we log off for half an hour till he's gone

(send Brent) good idea

Cleo: well guys, time for me to go. Bye.

Cleo [logout]

Brent [logout]

Jeremy: have a nice evening everybody

When I went to Echo school, I never dreamed I'd fall in love there. And with Jeremy Berg? Not in a million years!

I glanced again toward the man at the door. Why did the sight of him cause the blood to zoom around my body at twice its normal speed? I slid to the floor to sit closer to the computer. Jeremy took the couch space I'd vacated. I couldn't resist another look at him. "Uh-oh, danger," I heard a voice say in my head as lust possessed me like a creature from a horror movie. If I didn't watch out, he could interfere with the relationship I was developing with Brent. What was Jeremy doing at Echo school anyway? He'd been on Echo a year already. Had he come to meet me?

"Teach them banner," Jeremy shouted to Stacy.

"What's that?" someone asked.

"It enlarges words to full-screen size," Jeremy answered. "Go into my directory, Stacy, and cat the file Pub."

He's brilliant, I thought. Jeremy crossed his arms and I thought: Sexy, too, very sexy.

Confusion at Echo school ensued. Jeremy called out what sounded to us newusers like an incomprehensible string of words: "Type backslash, uh, backslash jeremy backslash pub."

The class deteriorated from there. Jeremy continued to disrupt us with examples of advanced computer commands that shot over our heads. He's showing off, I thought to myself. Instead of listening to the technobabble, the students conversed with each other.

Though this was my first experience in person, I'd already electronically met most of the people in the room. Despite being on CompuServe for several months, I'd never met anyone live. Unlike local Echo, CompuServe spanned the United States, Canada, Europe, and I'd even chatted with someone from Saudi Arabia. It amazed me how an image created by words on a screen differed from the person in flesh. To my right sat Sparkles, a woman I'd befriended both on Echo and on CompuServe's CB.

I turned to Sparkles and gave her a hesitant smile.

Though Sparkles and I had become best buddies online, I knew she hated me at first sight. Sparkles weighed around two hundred and fifty pounds and had short kinky hair. Her eyes bespoke loathing for my trim figure and blond-haired, blue-eyed, Barbie doll features. Just a week before, Sparkles had opened an item called "Fat and Beauty" that specifically decried Barbie as the ideal type. Online, I'd never pictured Sparkles as unattractive despite her mentioning being overweight, and I'm sure she'd never pictured me as a Barbie type.

Items in conferences constituted the main means of communication on Echo. Some began in 1990, the year of Echo's conception and continued sporadically whenever someone felt propelled toward the subject. Depressed Echoids poured out sorrow, the brokenhearted their pain, the exuberant their humor. Names attached to responses became real people, intimately known. Anyone could open an "item," a topic thread.

Now that Sparkles had met me in RL, I felt her hostility and had a hunch she'd never give me the one thousand sounds for my Mac computer as she'd promised.

I couldn't resist another look at Jeremy Berg. He smiled and pointed at my feet, always shoeless given the opportunity, and said, "You really do have an elephant tattoo."

I nodded and self-consciously fingered my earring. Only one of my ears was pierced, as I enjoyed lopsidedness. The earring dangled below my shoulder, and I was glad I'd dressed for the occasion in an off-the-shoulder blouse, though I could tell Sparkles resented it.

I told myself to be careful about Jeremy. Already in the midst of getting involved with Brent, I worried that these new feelings might interfere. I remembered Jeremy's bio said he was a single Jewish male, forty years old.

"How old are you?" Sparkles asked me.

"Forty-one," I answered.

"You're kidding! You look mid-twenties," she said, and I knew she hated me more than ever.

Echo school dispersed shortly after, partly because the crowd's attention had been lost.

Back home, I pondered the new shimmer the world had acquired during the evening. Lust, love, and sexual arousal budded in every cell in my body. But why for Jeremy Berg and why so suddenly?

NARAYAN! I realized.

He was Narayan.

Sixteen years before, in Bali, I'd been passionately in love with a thin man with short hair and glasses nicknamed Narayan. In those hippie days, short hair was an aberration and I'd berated myself for being attracted to someone with less than waist-long hair. But I was crazy for him anyway. The romance ended abruptly, though, the dreams of our future terminated. Now here was Narayan back again. I'd found him at Echo school, and the feelings had returned full force.

Though I'd written Jeremy off as a jerk when I'd communicated with him online, I, nevertheless, became instantly enamored with him because his appearance reminded me of an old boyfriend. The sight of him had triggered an "in love" switch. I wasn't in love with Jeremy. I was in love with Narayan, but the emotional memories of Narayan had been awakened and were now reassigned to someone else.

Throughout the next six years online, I found this phenomenon to hold true—the past colors the present. I've experienced and witnessed love affairs between people who'd never met in person or seen pictures of each other but who, from bits of former attractions, created idealized mental constructs of their cyber mate. The mind fills the void with the choicest selections.

Later that night I called an old friend. "I met Narayan tonight," I told her.

The morning after Echo school, I logged on as soon as I awoke. Echo had hooked me to where I felt compelled to visit it four times a day: morning, dashing home from the office at lunchtime, immediately after work, and then at least once before bedtime—a piddling amount of time to what I'd spent online a few years later.

I wrote email to Brent. I told him about the people I'd met at Echo school, people he, too, had yo-ed. He hadn't been able to attend because of an appointment.

I couldn't resist writing about Jeremy-Narayan. I explained how Echo school had gone awry because Jeremy Berg had interrupted it by showing off. I also noted that Jeremy was extremely smart. I felt like an infatuated teenager unable to stop talking about her love object as I rattled on about him. Later I worried that I'd exposed myself. Would Brent catch the love-lust for Jeremy in my tone?

After emailing Brent, I jotted a few messages to some of the people I'd met the night before: *Nice to have met you. Yo ya soon.* Sending and receiving email contributed to Echo's sense of community.

Mail finished, I typed *n* for new, to see the new responses added since I'd last logged on. "Central," the conference of entry, noted up-and-coming Echo events and contained items where people discussed immediate concerns. In "Shameless Self Promotion" I found out an Echoid was having an art show the following week, inviting all Echoids free. The next announced an article to be printed in that week's *New York Times* magazine. Echoids were a talented bunch, I thought, and felt proud to be one of them.

In the "Status Report" item, someone reported being grazed by a bicycle messenger and expressed fury that messengers went the wrong way down one-way streets. At the item's end, I typed *r* for response. The "Status Report's" format dictated you use your name at the beginning of every line. I wrote:

Cleo had a wonderful time at Echo school last night.
Cleo loved meeting Echoids f2f.

The online world uses abbreviations like f2f for face-to-face; btw for by the way; IMHO for In My Humble Opinion. In the same way that languages define cultures, bbs dialect shapes esoteric communality. Studies in sociolinguistics (e.g., Labov, 1984; Hymes, 1974) demonstrate how styles of speech denote particular social groups. My old flame Fire on CB had once sent me this ASCII (American Standard Code for Information Exchange) rose:

----<<--<@

Being avant-garde New York, some abbreviations used elsewhere, like LOL for Laughing Out Loud and ROFL for Rolling On Floor Laughing, were considered bad form on Echo. Symbols like ":)", representing a smiling face, and ": (", a frowning one, were also rejected as revealing an imagination too poor to express oneself properly.

I typed *o* to see who was online. Jeremy-Narayan was there. I felt a rush of excitement and yo-ed him, *Nice meeting you last night.*

He yo-ed back, *Ditto. Are you going to the Echo picnic next Sunday?*

I answered, *Yes.*

I didn't say I planned to go with Brent. I tried to remember previous yo's Jeremy and I had shared, before I'd met him—yo's I'd disregarded because I'd thought him an asshole. Once, Jeremy had mentioned his expertise at making popcorn. When I said I didn't cook, he declared he did, which I'd ignored as a come-on. Now the thought struck me: he's available for showing off his popcorn talent, and I warned myself again that this Narayan business could complicate things with Brent.

Jeremy Berg was not Narayan. Maybe he wasn't even as smart as I thought him to be. The knowledge anyone learned after a year on Echo would seem expert to a beginner. Was I projecting Narayan's charms onto Jeremy? I found myself unable to separate them. Narayan was long gone, one of the people who never made it out of Goa alive. Only my feelings for Narayan remained. Boy, did they ever! I was obsessed.

When a yo from Brent beeped onscreen, I felt irritated, resenting his interruption. Uh-oh, the kindled ardor for Narayan had already overshadowed my interest in Brent.

How to deal with these two? Jeremy and Brent. Or was it three? Jeremy, Brent, and Narayan.

Suddenly I heard *beep beep beep* and a message flashed on my screen: *Brent requests your presence in chat.*

Before joining him, I typed *o* to see if Jeremy was still on. He was. Not only didn't I want to chat with Brent, I didn't want Jeremy to see me doing it. I typed the command that provided a breakdown of which modem line the users were on, what time they'd logged in, and what they were doing. I noticed:

banana   ttym03 6:15am   yo jeremy

Banana was yo-ing Jeremy! I felt a twinge of jealousy. I also noticed that Brent was alone in chat, waiting for me. I felt trapped. I decided to bow out as quickly as possible.

Cleo: [login]
Brent: hi there
Brent: so how are you this morning?

Cleo: getting ready to leave actually. gottogo. Yo ya later

Cleo: [logout]

The no-longer-deniable lust for Jeremy-Narayan compelled me to revolt against Brent. I had no choice. My feelings for Jeremy-Narayan engulfed me. All I could think about was how to be with him. My brain didn't decide it. My soul decided—I yearned for Jeremy Berg.

No, I yearned for Narayan, but I wouldn't accept that fact for months to come.

With enough adrenaline in me to win the Kentucky Derby, I yo-ed Jeremy, *I'm waiting for the popcorn you said you'd make me.*

The pause before his answer unnerved me, though long pauses between yo's were the norm. If someone was reading through items, he or she often waited till everything new scrolled by. You could "Control-C" out of responses, but that could cause you to miss something. Long pauses and unanswered yo's didn't necessarily signify rudeness.

Finally he replied. *I'm rushing out to work. Leave me email about when you want to get together.*

And so began a ten-month-long relationship. With Echo's frequent f2f meetings—especially the one in a bar every other Monday night, which Jeremy and I never missed—we were soon an Echo couple.

From day one, little things Jeremy did annoyed me. Unfortunately, it took me months to realize he was not Narayan. Jeremy *was*, in fact, the social klutz I first thought he was. He continued to yo women during our relationship. He wasn't interested in dating them, he just didn't understand that you weren't supposed to flirt with your girlfriend's peers. One day a woman he invited to lunch declined his invitation. I was astounded when he told me about it that night.

"You invited her for lunch?" I asked, dying of hurt.

"Just as a friend. Only as a friend. You know I love you. If I wanted to see her as a date, I wouldn't be telling you about it, would I?"

What a jerk. The woman must have pitied me.

What finally made me see the light was when Jeremy's name turned up in WIT (Women In Telecommunications), the women-only conference. Under the item "Is Someone Bothering You on Echo?" a woman who didn't frequent the f2fs said Jeremy Berg was driving her crazy with yo's and invitations. Since she didn't go to Echo events, she didn't know he and I were in a relationship.

When I mentioned it to Jeremy, he was perplexed that someone could so misread his intentions. I believed his shock, having seen him behave ineptly in a variety of social settings. I'd also heard he was annoying the openly lesbian women in the group with his attentions.

That was the end of that. I finally accepted that the love I felt for Jeremy was really leftover from Narayan. And I had to admit that Jeremy didn't possess the intellect I'd originally swooned over. Narayan had been the brilliant one. Along with the love-lust that I'd attached to Jeremy, I'd also consigned him other qualities I'd cherished in Narayan. Though I'd been aware that first night that the feelings for Jeremy stemmed from old feelings for Narayan, it took me a year to separate the two individuals completely.

After the Jeremy Berg affair, I took the advice of KZ, the host of the Sex Conference on Echo: never date or mate with anyone on your local online service. It's like dating someone from your office—a recipe for disaster.

Echo had a men-only conference called MOE (Men On Echo). That ass Jeremy Berg once wrote in MOE a description of the delicious blow jobs his girlfriend gave him. He didn't mention my name, but everyone knew who his girlfriend was. Someone, whose identity I never confirmed but who could have been Brent, printed out Jeremy's post and sent it anonymously to my mother!

"Oh no, Momsy, Jeremy would never be so stupid as to write something like that for the whole world to see," was the only explanation I could give her. For Jeremy Berg, the term "village idiot" sprang to mind.

The image I'd held of Jeremy in my brain had been my own fabrication. The mental construct was just that—a construct, with varying pieces of reality and the rest made from the contents of my personal, historic spice shelf. I've seen this happen in online romances where the couple never meets; I've seen it in cross-cultural romances where they don't speak the same language; and I've seen it in RL, same-language, same-time-and-place relationships.

I'd never seen a picture of Fire or heard his voice on the phone. Yet I called it love and burned with lust for him. With Jeremy, I saw him, heard him, touched him, had my sexual needs satisfied by him, but was really interacting with Narayan. I called that love, too.

Our lives are a dizzying mishmash of past and present. The net brings these psychological entwinings into sharper focus. The prize is that we can learn from observing the tricks our minds play on us.

2. The Net/MOO-Sex

▶ My entry to the net also happened through Echo school. In the Internet Conference on Echo, I saw a thread about a chatlike thing called a MOO and another about an international, text-with-graphics thing called the World Wide Web. In 1994, I signed up for Echo Internet school. Echo had grown so much by that time that the classes were no longer held in Stacy's living room but at New York University.

Echo was in the process of making its own Web page, and though the equipment in the classroom was sophisticated, it was not up to showing us the Web. Stacy drew a dot on the board and called it Japan. "With the Web, if you click on a Japanese link on a Web page here in New York, you go instantly to Japan and get the information on a computer there."

Faster than an airplane, thought this world traveler. Oh boy. I was sold. When Stacy mumbled that she might give Echoids a free Web page, I jumped at the chance. I took her aside after class and said I wanted one—whatever it was.

That week I called Echo and asked to be shown "Mosaic," as Stacy had offered. She invited me to Echo, which was still in her apartment in those days, and she browsed me with Mosaic, which apparently she herself didn't know how to use well either. It was that new. With the warp-speed growth of the net, the term "Mosaic" vanished in a few months as news of "Netscape" passed from person to person and bbs to bbs, forcing everyone to either make the change or be left in the Stone Age of cyberspace.

During Stacy's demonstration of the Web, the bug bit me bad. On personal "homepages" I saw colorful photos of people with vignettes about themselves and drawings of their pets. How incredible it was—people could write something or paint a picture and make it available for the world to see. For the next two months I dedicated every free second to designing a Web page and learning to write in the computer language "html."

I started my Web page focusing on the research on prostitution I did in Thailand for my doctorate degree. My book *Patpong Sisters* was just coming out, and Patpong, the Bangkok red-light district, was fresh in my mind from a presentation I'd given at Hunter College, where I showed slides of the prostitutes I'd befriended. It stirred up memories of the Thai friends who had engaged three years of my life. When I heard that Web pages could have music, too, I bought a microphone and learned to encode a few bars of "One night in Bangkok and the world's your oyster. . . ." Were there copyright laws about using that? Who cared?

Web pages are spiced with colorful graphics, mostly "GIFs"—photos made viewable to a computer through the "Graphic Interchange Format." While deciding what

GIFs to have on my site, I struggled over a picture I had of a Patpong "Pussy Razor Blade Show." On Patpong, bars vied with one another to put on the most outrageous show, all involving things pulled out of, or manipulated by, a woman's vagina. Shows used Ping-Pong balls, cigarettes, horns, and one involved a naked woman pulling out a string of razor blades.

Could I put a picture of that on my homepage?

I wavered between yes and no. In the end I converted into a GIF a photo of a woman with her trailing string of razor blades and uploaded it to my page. I decided to use it because it was dawning on me that people in the United States couldn't have cared less about Thai prostitutes. They weren't interested in what went on outside their country. The mail I received from people who'd bought my book came from men who'd been to Thailand and knew about the prostitutes from firsthand experience.

I was sure the Razor Blade Show would be controversial, but it would also attract attention. That was my goal—first, to get people's attention and then to tell them about the heroic prostitutes who supported whole areas of the Thai countryside with their sexual labor.

Through my homepage, I wanted to present to the world the story of Patpong, a sleazy place that nevertheless provided its workers with a way to bring life to their villages. Many Patpong women came from Isan, the northeastern part of Thailand, where jobs were scarce or nonexistent. The only way to survive was for the area's young people to head for the cities, many ending up in Patpong.

During my research, I'd become so involved with the Patpong bar girls, I almost felt I was living their lives. At

Other jobs are so poorly remunerated that prostitution represents a rational choice in order to support their rural families. (Ong, 1985:5)

the end I was actually surprised one day to realize that I
wasn't a poor Thai who was going to lose her front teeth
because she couldn't afford a dentist. What a relief to reconnect to my American citizenship. The plight of the Thai
women remained part of me, though, and it became my
mission to have them recognized as heroines and not labeled as the scum of the earth for working in the sex
industry. According to a saying in Thailand, women are
"the hind legs of the elephant," meaning they drag passively behind the men who are the front ones (Schalbruch,
1988). I wanted the Patpong women to be recognized as
the front legs of the elephant.

It took some soul-searching to decide whether or not
to use the bar girls' photos and write about their private
lives in my book. I knew there was a chance someone
might feel hurt, betrayed, or shamed. In the end, though,
I decided that the important thing was to tell their stories.
I wanted history to remember and praise them.

So the Razor Blade Show was pictured prominently
on my homepage. Because the photo was fuzzy, beneath
it I wrote exactly what it depicted.

*The show starts with a woman appearing on
stage with a white slip over her chest reaching to*

below her crotch. In her hand is a piece of paper. She dances while pulling down the slip to expose her breasts. Next, she lifts the bottom and folds it around her waist, exposing her naked lower parts.

She dances some more before spreading her legs and bending over to insert her fingers into her vagina. She pulls out a razor blade on a string. She keeps pulling the string and out comes another razor blade . . . and another razor blade . . . and more razor blades.

Then, with one end of the string still inside her, she uses a blade to slice the piece of paper, thus verifying its sharpness. In this photo you can see the white slip bunched around her waist; the string with the razor blades; and the paper, which she hasn't yet sliced.

When I signed up for a PPP connection, the connection I needed for the web, I gained Internet access and sped into cyberspace. "Telnet" allows you to connect and interact with a remote computer. In between the hours I spent trying to figure out how to get the music to play on my homepage, I telneted to Lambda MOO and requested a character. MOOs grant, for free, a permanent "character" with your name of choice. After you receive the password at your email address, you can log on to the MOO for free, twenty-four hours a day, seven days a week, except for when the MOO is down for backups or if it crashes.

On a MOO, people log in from all over the world and

chat; whatever they type, be it *"I'm going to kill my neighbor"* to *"I want sex,"* will be immediately seen by everyone in the same MOO "room." At any one time there can be two hundred people doing different things in different places on the MOO. So in one room, Dingdong, calling from Malaysia, converses with Stingray who's in Ohio and Miraculix who's in Norway. In another room Fractal_Muse and Stormwatch declare their love for each other. Unfortunately, in RL, Fractal_Muse pined for her mate from California while Stormwatch pined from England. In her castle, PrincessC sat on a throne laughing with her MOO friends—in RL she was a teenage girl logging in from a hospital bed where she was dying of cancer.

Cyber sex is even more of a major attraction on the MOO than in other text-only spaces. The MOO is a giant step up in technological possibilities. What makes MOO sex special is the "emote" capability that allows you to portray an action such as "Henry blows snot out of his nose," plus the ability to write and program rooms and objects that remain permanently in the MOO's database. Lockable rooms can be locked so nobody else can enter, and many beds are programmed to respond to actions made on them, such as lying on one.

MOO sex is more interactive than hot chat. It's rich with imagery, involving more brain and less genitals. You can take off clothes, lie on furniture, and your actions reflect and adjust to that of your partner's. It's also less orgasm-oriented, though it is ultra-sensuous. The great masters of MOO sex, the ones who've been at it a long time, don't have pauses in their dialogue. The long pauses in hot chat indicate someone's hands are busy elsewhere.

> Don't let anyone tell you that there is no such thing as a cyber orgasm! (Albright: 14)

Sometimes people do reach climax in MOO sex and there may be pauses, but for the most part, the action is played out on cyber bodies, not real ones. It may seem odd to role-play with a *cyber* orgasm as a goal, instead of a *physical* one. Hundreds of MOOers, though, will attest to the satisfaction of this "completion," in its cerebral rather than corporal way.

Online love affairs naturally progress to online sex, but anonymous net-sexing is also a popular pastime. Having written a book about prostitution where I graphically described the sex shows I'd witnessed, it was easy for me to try out cyber sex. I had no problem going into a private room with someone and writing out the sex acts I was virtually engaging in. I easily typed the taboo words describing crude actions on our respective body parts. I could explicitly write *I am doing such-and-such with your so-and-so*.

The next step into net sex was harder. I had to consciously allow myself to go beyond my usual limits into sexual exploration. I had to step across a barrier I wouldn't normally even fantasize about much less consider doing. But once I saw how simple and nonrisky it was to explore new things in cyberspace, I gloried in trying out everything. A MOO allows you to log on as an anonymous guest and to describe yourself any way you want, as any gender you want.

Initially, MUD players appear to be neuter: automatically generated messages that refer to such a player use the family of pronouns including "it," "its," etc. Players can choose to appear as a different gender, though, and not only male or female. On many MUDs, players can also choose to be plural (appearing to be a kind of "colony" creature: "ChupChups leave the room, closing the door behind them"), or to use one of several sets of gender-neutral pronouns (e.g., "s/he," "him/her," and "his/her," or "e," "em," and "eir"). (Curtis)

With the freedom to be and do anything, I had sex with three men at once. I had sex with a woman. I had sex with three men and a woman at once. Posing as a man, I had sex with a woman. Posing as a gay man, I had sex with a man. Posing as a man, I had sex with a man who was posing as a woman. I learned all about S&M, as the sadist and as the masochist. I had all sorts of sex in every new way I could think of.

For a true MOOer, one MOO is not enough, especially if you start on Lambda, which is so famous for its "lag" we call it Lagda. "Lag" is a delay in response time due to Internet traffic or too many programs running at once. Usually, what you type is immediately seen on the screen, but with lag it could take from three to forty seconds, and on Lagda several minutes. Typically, MOOers "multi-MOO," having several windows open on the computer screen at one time, each for a different MOO. I can type a response in the Lagda window to my friend StarDancer, and during the minutes it takes to get her answer, I carry on a conversation with LMaui on Sprawl MOO and another conversation with The_Necromancer on Necro MOO.

After posing several times as a male, which entailed diligence in using gender pronouns for actions such as *puts his hand on your thigh*, I'd grown accustomed to double-checking before hitting the enter key. If I used *her hand* when I was supposed to be a male, I'd be in for trouble. After several sessions without mistakes, I felt reasonably confident that I could maintain the awareness of what went into which window and whether my body parts were his or hers.

I'm active on ten MOOs, but in the MUDDweller application folder on my hard drive, I have preprogrammed "macros" for different guest characters on Lambda, two female and one male, all set to log me in and set my gender and description. A preset key teleports me right into the Sex Room.

The MOO invites everyone to try out different genders and sexual preferences. Until only a few decades ago homosexuality was considered an aberration by much of society. "All psychoanalytic theories assume that adult homosexuality is psychopathologic." (Bieber, 1962:220) This has changed and many (Tisdale, 1995) now accept the Kinsey Report's premise of a range of sexual preferences, from 0 to 6, heterosexual to homosexual. Human sexuality is scattered across that range. On the MOO, we can go beyond preference, into curious exploration, without the RL pressure to commit to one end or another.

In the Sex Room, I found that what started as fun soon became compelling, even compulsive. I noticed this not only in myself but in the mob of other anonymous guests. Though they logged in as different guest characters each time (randomly, Purple_Guest or Red_Guest or Green_Guest), I could identify certain people by the language they used. One called everybody dear; one used the word "manhood" when she told someone to *put it in*. I saw the same people in the Sex Room day after day, hour upon hour, periodically pairing off (and orgying off) into private rooms before returning to the main room to find new partners. People also have sex openly in the Sex Room, cheered, joined, or ignored by the others present.

Lambda MOO has the most developed areas devoted to sex, and a @who listing of players reveals that about 25 percent are in one of the Sex Rooms. The "Den of Love" is a major hub, extending into private bedrooms.

The Den of Love—This tastefully furnished reception area is designated as a meeting place for people seeking consenting net-sex partners. The four playrooms adjoining this room are for the use of you and your partner(s). Type "green," "red," "blue," or "butterscotch" to enter one of the playrooms. Enjoy!

A reminder on Den policies: If you do not want to be interrupted or joined, PLEASE use the locks with which each Den playroom is equipped. The commands "lock here" and "unlock here" will control the lock. Not using the lock is a signal that joining you is okay. If you want privacy, please use the lock.

The Blue Room is NOT occupied and NOT locked. The Red Room is occupied and locked. The Green Room is occupied and locked. The Butterscotch Room is occupied and locked.

As female Olive_Guest, I typed *blue* to enter the Blue Room.

The Blue Room—You see a large room with interesting-looking furniture suited for playing. The floor is solid black granite, covered in places with thickly padded sculpted rugs with rich designs. The walls are granite of a salt-and-pepper color that contrasts nicely with the floor. Plants hang from the ceiling from steel chain holders that look stronger than they need to be.

In the center of the room is a four-poster full-sized bed. Leather straps are securely fastened around each post. The bedclothes look comfortable: sheets and a comforter of finely woven sapphire-blue silk. Type "@usage here" for instructions on using this room.

As usual, not long after I entered a bedroom, others followed.

Samah has arrived. Zappa has arrived. I say, "Hello." Zappa says, "Am I interrupting?" Copper_Guest has arrived. Copper_Guest says, "Hi all."

As Olive_Guest, I'd described myself as *too much for you*. After trying out various types of descriptions, I found that one to be the most provoking. *Zappa pages, "You seem like an interesting person." Samah [to Copper_Guest]: Hi. Olive_Guest shrugs. Copper_Guest pages, "Would you like to make love to another female?" Copper_Guest goes out.*

I couldn't decide if I wanted sex with any or all of the

males or what about Copper_Guest, the female? I paged Copper, *I'm not sure.* Zappa pages, *Sorry, you don't seem interested in me, hmm.* Copper_Guest pages, *Why not? I have a strap-on dildo. It would be the same as making love to a male.* I paged Copper, *Sounds interesting.*

I decided to @join Copper, who was in the Lady's Orgy Room.

Lady's Orgy Room: The first thing you notice are several restraints in the room and chains hanging from the ceiling. You smell the soft scent of sex from what went on here not long ago. In fact, you can almost hear the screams of pleasure bouncing off the walls. You notice a four-post bed with silky sheets. A sign on the south wall notes: NO MEN ALLOWED!!!!!

Copper_Guest says, "Hi Olive." Magenta_Guest says, "I'm 5'7", long brown hair, hazel eyes, 38-C chest. . . ." Copper_Guest says, "Wow, a threesome." I say, "Oh, hi." Copper_Guest says, "Join me, sweeties."

I typed: *sit on bed,* activating the "sit" verb on the bed, which outputted: *You pull back the top silk sheet of the bed and slip under it, feeling the fabric caress your skin.*

Magenta_Guest sat on the bed, too, which outputted: *Magenta_Guest pulls back the top sheet of the bed and slips under it, looking pleased and excited.*

Copper_Guest takes off her blouse and panties and says, "The rest is up to you two if you want your bra and panties to come off." I say, "Ooo." Magenta_Guest slowly and nervously removes her panties and T-shirt. Copper_Guest says, "My pussy is getting wet in RL." Copper_Guest says, "Magenta, you look gorgeous." Olive_Guest unbuttons her blouse.

I typed: *Look, Copper.*

Copper_Guest—a very sexy lesbian female with 38D breasts, a red bush, carrying a seven-inch strap-on dildo.

Copper_Guest says, "Magenta, come close to me and relax." Magenta_Guest blushes as she lies on her back. Copper_Guest slowly massages Olive's breasts. I say, "Ooo, that feels nice." Copper_Guest rubs Magenta's pussy gently. Olive_Guest puts her arms around Copper. Copper_Guest removes Olive's bra and panties. Magenta_Guest softly moans as her nipples get hard. Olive_Guest feels a warm glow in her groin. Copper_Guest slowly puts on her seven-inch strap-on and shudders as it touches her pussy. Matte_Guest tried to enter but was kept out by the locked door. Magenta_Guest has disconnected. The housekeeper arrives to remove Magenta_Guest. Copper_Guest asks, "Who will be the first to ride my fake cock?" I say, "Me, I guess, since Magenta left."

Copper_Guest asks, "Would you like to be eaten out?" I say, "I love that." Olive_Guest opens her legs. Copper_Guest says, "Well, sit on my face, hon." Olive_Guest gets on her knees and climbs on top of Copper's face. Olive_Guest strokes Copper's hair.

Copper_Guest slowly starts licking your pussy and biting your clit. Olive_Guest moans at the feel of Copper's tongue. Copper_Guest says, "You taste good." Olive_Guest moves her hips against Copper's face. Copper_Guest starts fucking you with her tongue. I say, "Ah, that feels nice." Copper_Guest says, "Do you like anal sex?" Olive_Guest groans as Copper's tongue goes in and out of her. I say, "Yes I do." Copper_Guest says, "Let me suck out your asshole." I say, "A dildo in my ass as you lick me sounds nice." Copper_Guest says, "Bend over and spread your ass and I'll fuck you with my strap-on." Olive_Guest turns over and sticks her butt in the air. Olive_Guest spreads her cheeks and says, "Fuck my ass."

Copper_Guest slowly shoves the fake cock in your tight ass and pumps harder and faster while fingering your pussy. I say, "Ah, that feels so good. Shove it all the way up." Copper_Guest shoves the whole cock in you, fucking you harder and deeper. Olive_Guest moans and moves back up against Copper so it goes in deeper.

Rosy_Guest teleports in. Copper_Guest pulls out of your ass and shoves very hard and deep into your cunt. (Though I'd suspected that Copper_Guest was male, this move convinced me. Egads, every female would shriek at the guaranteed E. coli infection, virtual or not.) I say, "Oh." Rosy_Guest says, "Hello? Am I interrupting anything?" Copper_Guest says, "Not at all, hon. Want to join us?" Rosy_Guest says, "I'd love to." I say, "Copper is fucking me with a dildo, but my tongue is hungry."

Rosy_Guest asks, "Where do you want me?" Copper_Guest says, "Come on, Olive, tell me you like it up your cunt." I say, "I love it in my cunt. Fuck me, Copper. Harder." Copper_Guest gives Olive a ribbed vibrator to use on Rosy. I say, "Rosy, come in front of me and spread your legs." Copper_Guest starts moaning with delight while fucking you harder and deeper. Rosy_Guest moves over to Olive and straddles her. Olive_Guest runs a finger over Rosy's cunt lips. Rosy_Guest says, "Mmm." Olive_Guest pumps her hips against Copper's dildo. Olive_Guest sticks her finger into Rosy and licks at her clit.

Copper_Guest says, "OLIVE, I'M GONNA CUM IN RL I FUCK YOU FASTER HARDER AND DEEPER."

Rosy_Guest moans with delight. Olive_Guest sticks her finger deeper into Rosy and runs the dildo head over Rosy's clit. Copper_Guest rolls over and says, "Ladies, please lick my cum-soaked pussy." Copper_Guest has disconnected. The housekeeper arrives to remove Copper_Guest.

I knew without a doubt that female Copper_Guest had been a male. "Lick my cum-soaked pussy" indeed! No wonder the lesbian rooms were so popular. I teleported to the Sex Room.

The Sex Room—You find yourself in a place created solely for pleasure! This is a public place without locks. You may use this room whenever you want, but don't expect privacy. It's built for making love, and its description is limited only by your imagination. Leave your inhibitions at the door! Part of the fun of this room is that others can watch and take part, too! Enjoy!

Members Only is to the east. The Den of Love is to the west. A door leads south to Sensual Respites. Cyan_Guest is here.

I typed south to go to Sensual Respites.

Sensual Respites—Torches are set into ornate metal holders along the oddly angled, gray stone walls. Smoke fills the room, mingling with the erotic smells of sex and stale perfume. Several stages form a semicircle at the far end of the room. There is a large open area in front of the stages, and sofas and lounges line the walls.

Type "help here" for features and commands on this room. Exits lead north to the Sex Room, northwest to the

Den of Love, east to the Lady's Orgy Room, west to the Romance Chamber, up to MagickMan's House of Porn, and down to the Dungeon.

No one is currently on any of the stages. In the audience: Female: Lavender_Guest, Mauve_Guest, Grenade, Roulette, LoveSearch, Camilla, and Olive_Guest. Male: Repo_Man, Brown_Guest, Lucas, Zaphod, Satan, Fawn_Guest, Jewish_Prince, and Blues-Singer.

Zaphod grins. Camilla smiles. Mauve_Guest teleports out. Camilla [to Repo_Man]: Hello, again . . . Lucas pages, "With a description like that, you're too much for anyone . . . since it's nonexclusive . . . why should anyone bother?" Repo_Man says to Camilla, "Hello there!" NorthStar teleports in.

I paged Lucas: *"Please don't, then." Lucas has received your page. NorthStar waves. Lucas pages, "Haha. Gladly." You feel a hot tingling on the back of your neck and your body shakes slightly. A small goblinoid man runs into the room, grins at you, and hands you a piece of paper. "Satan is lookin for ya," he gurgles, and then disappears. Satan pages, "Too much for even me? I don't think so."*

Camilla waves to NorthStar. Zappa enters from the Sex Room, a smile on his face. Repo_Man notices Lavender_Guest looking at him, and waves.

I looked at Satan—*He is tall and quite thin and smiles as you look at him. He has bleached blond hair that contrasts his dark eyebrows, and two small horns protrude from his hair. Despite the raunchy name, he seems quite friendly. Deep blue eyes meet your gaze unflinchingly.*

Satan's bare chest is thin but finely toned. Dark blond pubic hair leads a small path down to his large erect cock, which bobs slightly as air passes over it. His legs are long and thin, finely muscled.

Olive_Guest waves to Satan. Satan wiggles his toes at Olive. Olive_Guest winks at Satan. Lavender_Guest whines.

Zappa leaves for the Den of Love. René enters from the Sex Room, a smile on her face. Satan licks his lips and winks back. Satan yawns, looks at his watch, sprouts black, leathery wings, and suddenly departs from your presence, making you miss him so much it hurts.

Repo_Man hugs Camilla warmly. Satan pages, "What's up?" Yellow_Guest waves hello.

I page Satan: "Not much." A small, hairless dog runs up to you, licks you all over, and eats your message in a sloppy gulp. He looks up at you, grins, and says, "Satan should get this as soon as it passes through my system." He then grunts and leaves, trailing saliva as he goes.

Brown_Guest naughtily tries to sneak into Members Only, but is turned away at the door. LoveSearch winks. Blues-Singer waves to you. A crystalline butterfly flies through the room, circling around Grenade, momentarily distracting her from the conversation. Olive_Guest giggles. LoveSearch goes east. A man saunters into the room wearing silver boots. Spanker says, "Okay! I'm back!"

Blues-Singer steps onto Stage 1.

<1> Blues-Singer [sings]: "I got the blues baby, those low-down Lambda MOO blues. . . ."

Green_Guest climbs up the stairs from the Dungeon.

Green_Guest pages, "Hi there." Yellow_Guest pages, "Do you want to feel good?" I say, "Hi, Green." I page Yellow, "I always want to feel good."

<1> Blues-Singer [sings]: Early this morning . . .

<1> Blues-Singer [sings]: A sexy chick-guest made me erect.

<1> Blues-Singer [sings]: I get to her hot spot . . .

<1> Blues-Singer [sings]: And all she could do was disconnect!

<1> Blues-Singer [sings]: We got the blues, baby, those Lambda MOO blues. . . .

Jewish_Prince says, "Woo! Go Blues-Singer!" Olive_Guest giggles. Yellow_Guest pages, "So do you want to go somewhere and chat?"

<1> Blues-Singer [sings]: Whenever I get horny . . .

<1> Blues-Singer [sings]: and I find me a chick . . .

<1> Blues-Singer [sings]: I get us a private room . . .

<1> Blues-Singer [sings]: Only to find out she's got a dick. . . . I got the blues, baby . . . those low-down LambdaMOO blues. . . .

Blues-Singer causes Fawn_Guest to fall down laughing. Jewish_Prince laughs at Blues-Singer. Fawn_Guest says, "That is so funny!"

<1> Blues-Singer [sings]: I ain't got no money . . .

<1> Blues-Singer [sings]: Ain't got a car. . . .

<1> Blues-Singer [sings]: I can't even find a Woman . . .

<1> Blues-Singer [sings]: Just a guy playing with a different gen-Dar. . . . I got the blues, baby . . . those gender-crossin' . . . Lag eating . . . no loving . . . no talking . . . low-down, dirty Lambda MOO blues!

<1> Blues-Singer plays the final riff on his guitar. . . .

<1> *Blues-Singer takes a bow.*
<1> *Blues-Singer steps off Stage 1.*

Repo_Man applauds Blues-Singer. Olive_Guest [to Blues-Singer]: How did you find out about the dick? Loree has a mind-blowing, screaming orgasm that is heard throughout the MOO.

Blues-Singer [to Olive_Guest]: She/he told me while I was in her/his ass. . . . I immediately took her/his hands and put them in the leather restraints and I pulled out a knife and I chopped it off ;)

Olive_Guest giggles. Blues-Singer [to Olive_Guest]: I don't go for Oscar Mayer wieners ;) Green_Guest teleports out. Blues-Singer [to Faun_Guest]: So you see, I am a godly male type of man. Olive_Guest [to Blues-Singer]: I don't have a wiener. Blues-Singer [to Olive_Guest]: You don't? Would you mind if I inspected and saw for myself ;) Olive_Guest [to Blues-Singer]: Sounds like fun. Olive_Guest pulls up her skirt for Blues and pulls her panties down for a second. Blues-Singer [to all]: See, flirting is not dirty, and all should be able to see the flirtations of others so we can learn. Blues-Singer looks hard at Olive's pelvis . . . his eyes look up and down. . . . Nope, NO weenie there ;)

Red_Guest teleports in. Olive_Guest looks at Blues' crotch for hint of a bulge. Red_Guest says, "Any chick want to blow me?" Sivart enters from the Sex Room, a smile on his face. Roulette says, "Gee, he's direct :)" Blues-Singer gives Red a chick that will blow. So what if it's made of latex and is a little worn. It will still do the job :) Sivart leaves for the Den of Love. Red_Guest says,

"Any chick that is of female human origin, and living, preferably with teeth?"

Blues-Singer [to Red_Guest]: Teeth are a good thing. Red_Guest [to Blues-Singer]: I know, but it's not a necessity for head. Blues-Singer hands Red a (7-year-old woman with saggy breasts and dentures. . . . She hasn't blown anything in years and she wants to try. Magenta_Guest teleports in. Blues-Singer bonks his typist onna head!

Blues-Singer [to Red_Guest]: That was supposed to be a 97-year-old woman! I say, "7? Uh-oh." Red_Guest [to Blues-Singer]: Thanks for your help, but I don't think we have the same picture in mind, you pedophile! Blues-Singer takes his typist by the cock and spins him around his head. . . . He lets go and we all hear, "Aoooooooooo!"

Blues-Singer causes Roulette to fall down laughing. Olive_Guest slaps at Blues for being a pedophile. Red_Guest says, "Any lady (living) want to blow me?" Olive_Guest giggles. Blues-Singer says, "97, 97, 97, 97!" Magenta_Guest climbs down the stairs to the Dungeon. Olive_Guest [to Blues-Singer]: I understood ya. Don't worry.

Blues-Singer [to Olive_Guest]: I said 97, I hit the (instead of the 9, I used the shift key by mistake! Red_Guest climbs down the stairs to the Dungeon. Blues-Singer pulls out a Super Soaker squirt gun and takes aim at Olive_Guest. Blues-Singer pulls the trigger and squirts Olive_Guest in the middle of the chest, soaking her clothes.

I say, "Eeek." Blues-Singer [to Olive_Guest]: That's for slapping me ;) Hey, did anyone ever tell you that you *look darned good in a wet T-shirt? Blues-Singer [to Ol-ive_Guest]: Yes, you are all woman ;) Ecru_Guest has arrived. Olive_Guest [to Blues-Singer]: Oh gee, now you can tell I'm not wearing a bra. Spanker climbs down the stairs to the Dungeon. Magenta_Guest climbs down the stairs to the Dungeon.*

Ecru_Guest asks, "Anyone up for a gang bang?"

MOOers can create a "child" of a "generic" object. The defining quality of a MOO is that a "child" object shares the programs that exist on the generic "parent" object. One of the most popular generic MOO objects is the "clothing." You create a child of this object and name it what you want—a hat, a sweatsuit, a garter belt. After you describe it—*a sombrero with an Aztec pattern around the brim,* or *black lace crotchless undies*—you can set its "coverage" message, which designates the part, or parts, of the body it covers: head, neck, chest, groin, legs, or feet. The generic clothing comes with the ability to be worn; its verbs (commands) are "wear," "remove," and "strip." My first MOO name was "Patpong." If I created a *red bra* and typed *wear bra,* the screen would announce *Patpong puts on a red bra.* If I gave permission for Quinn to strip me, he could type *strip bra from Patpong* and the screen would say: *Quinn removes Patpong's red bra.*

Quinn was the creator of the generic clothing, and, in fact, I'd let him strip me more than once. Though some people want to be anonymous online, others point you to their homepages, where they provide photos and in-depth secrets about themselves. I'd seen Quinn's homepage. He was a full-fledged cutie pie, twenty-three years old, long hair, gorgeous body. He could have *strip*-ed me anytime he wanted.

I've later taken transcripts of the physically orgasm-less MOO sex scenes and replayed them as masturbation fodder. The logs of my encounters with Quinn were especially delicious.

When I entered a MOO romance, I weaned myself off of anonymous guest sex, but I know how irresistible it can be. The prudish fanatics who want to censor the net would faint if they knew what really happened online. Porn pictures are nothing compared with the events in a Sex Room. But in truth, it's just a window into human sexuality. Moreover, there's no stopping the evolution of net sex. Like bringing CNN to a country where women are veiled and told they aren't capable of self-determination—once the medium exists, people will realize its, and their, potential. Through CNN, Muslim women saw that in other countries women drove cars, flew fighter planes, and charged Supreme Court nominees with sexual harassment. In the same way, the Internet is bringing sex into people's homes, laying it right in their laptops.

The special thing about cyber lust, because it's presented through text, is that you can observe it as an isolated thing, as if you were holding an object in your hand: "This is my lust. And here's what it looks like." You are forced to recognize that it resides within each of us. It's part of being alive.

It's not easy to find an anonymous sex partner. I've gone into the Sex Room anticipating a quickie with anyone but ending up turned off by all. I thought the personlessness of a guest would cut out the search for the perfect someone of the right age, weight, clothing style, and facial appearance. It doesn't. It's almost as hard to find a virtual partner on a MOO as it is to find a real person at a party. Personalities show through, and men can say the exact words that turn me off or they don't say the ones that turn me on. Sexual competence is also a major factor for an ongoing online affair.

After discovering the expansive aspects of MOO sex I decided never again to resort to the low-quality cyber sex of hot chat. Whenever I'd hankered for anonymous MOO sex and went to a Sex Room, I was turned off by the obvious signs of a hot-chatter, such as *"What are you wearing?"* In hot chat, both parties masturbate while occasionally writing something to the other person. The words degenerate to long pauses in dialogue as each does his or her thing on his or her self. Hot chat relies on picturing the real person, hence asking questions like *What do you look like?* and *How big are your tits?* instead of using imagination.

At the beginning of an affair with a MOO man named Tomato, I'd still been fascinated with net sex and sometimes had two windows open to Sex Rooms on Lambda. I'd be a male guest in one and a female in another. During those times I was vigilant about typing in the wrong window. There was no way I could have explained to Tomato when, as Green_Guest, I typed: *Green_Guest slips her tongue into Beige_Guest's ear and says, "Come to a private room with me"* if I entered it into Tomato's window by mistake. He would have realized I was Green_Guest seducing Beige_Guest in another room.

One day Tomato told me, *I made special Web pages just for you,* and gave me the "url," the Web address.

I moved aside the MOO window and opened Netscape to go to the page. I found a picture of him in his living room. *Click on the clothes to remove them,* he told me. *Or click on my side to turn me around.*

I clicked on his pants and sure enough they came off. A new picture loaded, this time of him in green boxer shorts. I clicked on the shorts. Wowee, there was my Tomato, shirt on, naked penis hanging down, seductive smile on his face.

I switched to the MOO window and wrote: *Woo woo* before hurrying back to the Web. After I turned him around to see his naked butt, I turned him back and clicked off his shirt. When he was totally naked, I went back to the MOO and said, *Wow, that's great.*

Don't stop, he whispered. *Get me hot.*

Back on the Web, I clicked on his penis and received a new picture. He lay on the floor, holding himself, now hard and erect.

Hey! I asked. *Who took these pictures?*

Don't get jealous. I did them myself. The camera has a five-second delay. You know I'm all yours. Keep going.

The more I clicked, the closer the camera zoomed in and the less of Tomato was in the picture. Soon, a giant cock took up the whole screen.

Oh boy, oh boy, I said to him quickly before returning to the photo. The last click revealed his full body with an orgasmic expression on his face and a huge glob of sperm shooting in the air.

Yikes! How on earth did you get that shot? You snapped it, hurried into position, and came exactly after the five-second delay?

He laughed. *I have to admit, I used PhotoShop to touch that one up.*

His wasn't the first male organ I'd seen online, nor was it the first time I'd seen his. Tomato had sent me a GIF early in our relationship. To take it, he'd stayed late at his office. After everyone left, he put pencils under the door to prevent the cleaning crew from entering unexpectedly then pulled down his pants and sat on the scanner.

He converted the scanned picture to a GIF and e-mailed it to me. Erotic, it wasn't. His balls had flattened against the glass and the veins in his penis bulged like gargantuan termite trails. But I appreciated the effort and had a good giggle picturing him sitting naked on the office scanner.

Others, too, had sent me GIFs of their jewels, some without their faces or telling me their names.

On a MOO, you write programs to make your fantasy objects do whatever you want. I've always loved programming, so when I discovered the MOO I was ecstatic. I feel a rush when I get a program to work after hours of battling error messages. The solving of each little mistake gives me a thrill, then when the whole thing runs to completion—WOW! The pleasure is equal to any runner's high I've experienced. The MOO intensifies the rapture even more because it accesses my fantasies at the same time. Then other MOOers interact with my inventions, bringing them to life.

My main MOO after Lambda is Sprawl. My theme on Sprawl MOO is a red-light district. With Patpong fresh in my mind when I created, and had to name, my first MOO room, the words "Patpong Bar" popped into mind. A bar owner! Hey, I could be a bar owner.

For all the drugs I consumed during my hippie years in Goa, their negative effects may have been less than the emotional scars left from three years in Thailand. Sexism has left the most devastating imprint on me, but it took cyberspace to make me realize it. Though I was in Thailand as a researcher, observing from the sidelines, I was nonetheless in the center of events, taking in stimuli and processing them within myself, changing my perception of the world, changing my perception of gender relations.

One genre of Patpong bars I studied was the "blow-job bar." Patpong is a tourist spot, and the majority of patrons are Western men, called *farangs* in Thailand. As in the other bars, I formed a relationship with one of the employees of the Rose, a blow-job bar, and I followed her life for the next few years that I stayed in the country. Her name was Dang.

I didn't have to ask questions to find out Dang was twenty-three and had been working there two years. All the girls in the Rose came from Udon, in the Northeast, and had heard about the job from each other. The female owner was herself from Udon and also owned the Kangaroo next door (another sex-on-the-spot bar). Dang pointed out her "older sister," who'd taught her the trade.

When three *farang* men came up the stairs, Dang moved me to the couch against the wall. The other girl wrapped her arms around one of the men.

Two blow jobs commenced. One man sat at the far corner of the bar. A hostess, with the top of her dress pulled down, unzipped his pants and bent over to take his penis in her mouth. Her head pumped up and down and the hand that held his penis moved vigorously. The man frequently looked down to watch her. Then he'd gaze casually at the bar. The hostess worked without breaking stride, slowing down, or changing position for seventeen minutes. I wondered if my presence made it take longer than usual. When the man ejaculated, she unrolled a few sheets of toilet paper from the many rolls that lined the bar and cleaned him up. Then she refastened her dress.

At the same time, another *farang* was being serviced on the couch. One girl kneeled on the floor between his legs fellating him, while another kneeled on the couch to his left offering her breast to his mouth. When he ejaculated, the girl on the floor cleaned him up with toilet paper. I noted: lots of toilet paper; no condoms. Meanwhile, Dang's friend had escorted her *farang* to sit on the other side of Dang and she crouched on the floor between his legs.

Since Dang was seated between me and the action, I had a front-row view of events. Dang chattered; I watched. I barely heard a word she said. I wanted to go to the Ladies' Room to write but a kneeling girl blocked the way. (Odzer, 1994:53-54)

After leaving the bar, I contemplated my reaction, and have since discovered this corroboration:

What did I feel? Angry with the men? Maybe a bit. Sorry for the girls? Maybe that too. Jealous that men had this sort of thing available to them? Yes, very. And what else? Elated that I'd entered this strange world. Excited that I was trespassing into male territory. Resentful that being serviced by a woman was considered male sexuality. And even more resentful that women didn't have this same right to sexual gratification. (Ibid.:54)

So I created the Patpong Bar. In Thailand, I'd interviewed American men who lounged all day in their tropical bars, surrounded by adoring women awaiting their attention. They viewed it as paradise. Me, they treated as a female (meaning misfortunately gendered) who could only sigh wistfully at their good luck. Now I could be a bar owner, too. Ha!

After the bar, I created prostitutes and then a whole Patpong Road, named after the road in Bangkok. I named myself Patpong on Sprawl, too.

To learn MOO programming, I took the online tutorial that explains the basics of the language by teaching you how to make a windup duck. Step-by-step, it details how to program the duck so you can wind it, drop it, then watch it spin and quack. With the MOO being text-only, the "watching" occurs only in mental imagery. From yduJ's MOO Programmer's Tutorial:

First, we need some way to tell if the toy has been wound up. We'll create a property called "wound" on the toy.

@property toy.wound 0

Property added with value 0.

Before we can write our program, we need a verb. . . . We want to give commands like "wind duck" so we give it an argument list of "this." The variable "this," when used inside a verb, refers to the actual object (e.g. the duck) on which the verb called. Its place in the argument list designates how the verb will be found by the built-in parser.

@verb toy:wind this

Verb added.

Now we can make a simple program to wind the toy.

```
@program toy:wind
this.wound = this.wound + 2;
player:tell("You wind up the", this.name, ".");
player.location:announce(player.name,
"winds up the " ,    this.name, ".");


@program duck:continue_msg
times = {"once", "twice",
"thrice"}[random(3)];
return "swivels its neck and quacks " + times
+ ".";
```

If I typed *wind duck* and *drop duck*, others in the room would see on their screen: *Patpong winds the duck. Patpong places the duck on the floor. The duck swivels its neck and quacks two times. The duck swivels its neck and quacks once. The duck swivels its neck and quacks thrice.*

To fit the Patpong Bar, I created "Nok the Prostitute" modeled on the duck, and I programmed her to perform oral sex. I never consciously planned to open a whorehouse; I grasped at what I thought was a fun idea to inspire me through the twelve-page tutorial. I thought it ironic to be a virtual bar owner and to own prostitutes, but I wasn't totally conscious of what I was role-playing, or of the psychological thirst I was quenching.

Instead of the "wind" command, I gave Nok a "pay" command. To run my creation, therefore, you'd type *"pay Nok"* rather than *"wind duck."* The tutorial described how to make the duck quack a random number of times: once, twice, or thrice. For her sex act, I randomized Nok's tongue movements so she'd twirl her tongue either "vigorously," "slowly," or "round and round."

Several types of things exist on the MOO, for example: players, rooms, doorways, containers, and objects. A room comes with specific characteristics. So the Patpong Bar, because it's a room, allows players to go inside it, to witness what happens there, and to interact with things and other people. Upon entrance, a player sees a description of the room. The Patpong Bar is described as *A comfy room with couches around the walls.* The player also sees who else is in the room. I'm usually there, so the player will see my name. Because the bar is my designated "home," when I log off, my character stays there and anyone coming in would see me with the message *(asleep).* They would also see the objects I put there: Nok the Prostitute, Chai the Prostitute, and Lek the *katoey* (one female, one male, and one *katoey*, which is a Thai combination of male and female). A room can have doorways, so from the Patpong Road room you can go to one of my three other rooms: north to the Patpong Bar; east to the Pussy Galore Bar; west to the Boy Toy Bar; or south to Micro Avenue—a main road of Sprawl MOO, which is laid out like a city.

Some objects, such as doorways, come with preset "verbs". The default for a doorway is *You enter the such-and-such room,* depending on the room's name; but you can customize what someone sees when they use a doorway. Upon entrance into the Patpong Bar, a player sees: *Nok the Prostitute smiles at you and says, "Come on in, honey."*

If someone types, *Look Nok,* they see the description

I gave her: *I am a nineteen-year-old woman from Ubon Ratchatani. Order me, then pay me, and I will perform oral sex on you.*

Look Lek, on the other hand, gives the description: *I am a twenty-nine-year-old woman, uh, man . . . no, woman, from Phuket. Actually, I'm a katoey. Order me, then pay me, and I will perform oral sex on you.*

I'd originally assigned the *katoey* another name, but in a snippy mood, I changed it to Lek when I found out that Lek was the name of the Thai girlfriend of a journalist named Peter who coauthored a book about Bangkok prostitutes. Through mutual friends we began emailing each other after my book came out. Though we'd never met in person, I'd formed an emotional attachment to him, and when I heard he had a Thai girlfriend, I sought revenge by changing the *katoey*'s name to Lek. During my research in Thailand, not only did I have to deal with Western men's view of the country as their male haven, I also heard over and over how Western men preferred the sweet, docile Thai women to their American counterparts. So I was doubly annoyed to find out about Peter's Lek. I was doubly amused to name the *katoey* Lek. It's a joke among Bangkok's expat residents that the uninformed heterosexual male tourist who visits Thailand and buys a lady companion for the night wakes up sober the next morning to find himself snuggling someone with a deep voice, huge feet, an Adam's apple, and beard stubble on her face. A percentage of Patpong prostitutes are *katoeys* and they look beautifully feminine to the untrained eye.

During my research in Thailand, I was caught in the middle of two wildly differentiated groups and I identified with both—the privileged Western men with enough cash to see the Third World and its people as a commodity, and the Patpong women, arranged in the minds of Thai and Western men as something less than human, who weren't expected to have wants and desires of their own. Stretched between these dual universes, some part of me tore. The MOO helped me mend.

The MOO is also a great way to expel hostility in creative ways. I remember giggling as I changed the *katoey*'s name to Lek. When Peter emailed me, *"Can you please call the* katoey *something else? I want to show Lek the Internet but don't want her seeing that."*

I emailed back: *"No. Hahaha."*

With sex being a prime mover, online and off, the most frequent "search" done on the Web by fun seekers concerns sex-related topics. Many people find my Web page by using a "search engine"—which searches the Web— for the word "pussy." Thanks to my Pussy Razor Blade Show, my page comes up high on the list of pussy finds.

Eventually, some people in Thailand found it and a Bangkok newspaper complained about "Virtual Sleaze in Cyberspace":

> Thailand's notorious flesh trade means that it comes as no surprise that the country should be featured in the pornography corners of the Internet. . . . Among the more unusual finds can be

counted the home page of Cleo Odzer. . . . (Paroite, 1995)

When I started playing with html, I linked GIF pictures
of the prostitutes I'd befriended in Thailand to their robot
counterparts. Then, proud of my accomplishments, I
linked the brothel to my homepage. I also created a hot
spot on the page. This opened a telnet application that
would take a visitor straight from Netscape into a telnet
window open to Sprawl MOO. Included were instructions
on how to log in as a "guest," plus details on how to get
to the Patpong Bar.

In addition to the magnetic pull of the word "pussy,"
hundreds of people a day visited my page because I'd
listed myself in several Web directories as "Cleo the MOO-
flower Madam." In a magazine article about me:

What does the one and only Mayflower Madam
think of all this? "Sounds like fun," says Sydney
Biddle Barrows. "Is virtual 'madaming' profitable?" (Quan, 1995:35)

An endless stream of thrill seekers visited my Internet
brothel. When I spent evenings and weekends in the Patpong Bar, I'd receive one new guest about every ten
minutes. They logged in from Europe, Singapore, and even
Korea. I'd wave to them, say hi, and ask which gender of
prostitute they'd like. Then, after telling them what command to type, I'd watch their chosen prostitute drop to
his or her knees, do the work, and smile up at the recipient

when the program announced that the customer had achieved orgasm. Fortunately, my employees got the job done in a few seconds or the monotony would have killed me. Excluding the line breaks that occur after each sentence, hundreds of times I watched:

Pine_Guest orders Nok the Prostitute. Pine_Guest pays Nok the Prostitute. Nok the Prostitute drops to her knees and exposes Pine_Guest's genitals. Nok the Prostitute licks Pine_Guest's genitals and swirls her tongue round and round. Nok the Prostitute licks Pine_Guest's genitals and swirls her tongue vigorously. Nok the Prostitute licks Pine_Guest's genitals and swirls her tongue softly. Nok the Prostitute smiles with satisfaction as Pine_Guest comes.

Visitors frequently asked me, "Why are you running a virtual brothel?", a question I had to ponder. I concluded that after doing sex-industry research in Thailand for three years, I had to resolve some issues of control over my environment. The MOO is great for working out emotional troubles. You can create a scene you need to psychologically explore and rescript it any way you want, in as many ways that you want. After so many years in Thailand passively observing the sale of women, I craved the chance to relive the scenario with myself in charge. The MOO gave me that opportunity. Without realizing it, I had reinvented a memory that needed fixing and replayed it with a gratifying outcome. The part of me that had split in the research—identifying with both the Western men and the Patpong women—came together as I merged them in cyberspace. They'd found a place where they could coexist within me without clashing.

To answer Sydney Biddle Barrows, the Mayflower Madam—no, virtual madaming is not profitable in monetary terms. The reward comes in psychological ones.

After a while I was sick to death of watching the virtual prostitutes go into action, but by then I felt as though a mental burden had been lightened. Somehow, while directing Orange_Guest and Pear_Guest and Pine_Guest on how to get their virtual rocks off, I'd achieved closure. The powerless observer had gained control over the prostitution industry. In effect, the MOO provided me with an arena where I was able to restore the balance upset by years of research into men's sexual entertainment.

And since I could control what went on in my bar, I was no longer a passive observer. Sometimes I'd get an obnoxious guest who wanted cyber sex with me, not just with my robots, so I made attack programs to deal with people who annoyed me. I could make them virtually bleed, I could eject them from the bar, give them hiccups, make them sneeze and fart.

Women's-rights advocate that I am, after the Patpong Bar, I created a Boy Toy Bar with bikinied go-go boys and I declared it *for women only*. Inside the Boy Toy, I programmed a gigolo to describe his sexual prowess to any female player who activated him. Rather than the short script of the prostitutes, I wanted the gigolo to take his time and present a vivid picture of his cunnilingus talent. Originally, I'd named the gigolo Peter, since at its time of creation, I'd been flirting in email with Peter the author, and he'd had even offered suggestions, one of which was "tastes like strawberries." Soon, though, he chickened out, worrying about his internationally acclaimed *nom de plume*, since I also mentioned the title of his book. So I renamed the gigolo Dan Quayle. Anyone who typed *pay Dan* was subject to a step-by-step account of what Dan Quayle was doing to her intimate body parts. I altered it to fit its new name—a change in the gigolo's looks and the use of "potatoe" instead of "strawberries."

Typing *Look Dan* gave the description: *He's not too bright but he's sexually proficient. If you're a female, try him out. Type: pay Dan and he'll bring you to ecstasy.*

After paying Dan, a player would see on her screen, with enough pauses between each line to read one sentence at a time:

Dan Quayle places his hand inside your blouse and cups your breast. Dan Quayle lowers his lips to your breast and sucks on the nipple. Dan Quayle moves his other hand up the inside of your leg and rubs your crotch. Dan Quayle continues to suck your nipple as he lowers your panties. Dan Quayle caresses your pussy softly, teasing you with his fingers. Dan Quayle slides the tip of one finger into you as his knee pushes your legs open. Dan Quayle teases your clit with his thumb as he inserts his finger farther. Dan Quayle gives your nipple one last flick with his tongue before he moves his head to your crotch. Dan Quayle breathes close to your pussy. You feel his warm breath on your insides. Dan Quayle gets on the floor between your legs as he lowers his lips to your clit. Dan Quayle says "Mmmmmmm," and exclaims, "Tastes like potatoe!" Dan Quayle pushes his finger deep inside you as he licks your clit. Dan Quayle pumps his finger in and out, as his tongue twirls in circles. Dan Quayle inserts a second finger into you and increases the intensity of his pumping. Dan Quayle flicks wildly at your clit with his tongue and says, "Let me know when you're coming, my big big honey, so I can get it all in my mouth." Dan Quayle swipes his tongue in circles over and around your clit, pumping hard, fast, and deep with his fingers. Dan Quayle buries his face in you as his tongue sweeps madly and his fingers dive in and out. Dan Quayle senses you're about to come, and when he hears you moan, he changes his tongue to a back-and-forth motion, pumping his fingers in a steady rhythm. Dan Quayle groans with happiness when you yell, "OHHHHHHH!" Dan Quayle senses that your climax has ended. Dan Quayle licks all around your pussy, sucking every drop, licking the inside of your thighs as well. Dan Quayle raises his head and smiles. Dan Quayle says, "Sawat dee ti rak," and moves away.

"Sawat dee ti rak," means "good-bye, my love" in Thai, a leftover from the Peter gigolo.

One day while escaping my virtual red-light district on Sprawl MOO, I cruised the Sex Room on Lambda MOO as the anonymous Purple_Guest, describing myself as a brunette dressed in overalls. (In reality, I wouldn't be caught dead in overalls.) At that moment I needed to be someone else. I never entered the Sex Room in my normal character, having the reputation of my persona to protect. But

> The physical aspect . . . may be only virtual, but the emotional aspect is actual. (Reid, 1991)

as a guest, I could do any wild and weird act I could think of and be anyone I wanted. A week earlier I'd been a gay male, and in a private room with another male, I'd discovered some interesting facts about gay sex. This day I met Jagwire, who described himself as a tanned blond surfer in spandex shorts.

Jagwire said to me, *You're really one of those people that has a character but comes to the Sex Room to play around as a Guest, aren't you?*

His simple statement intrigued me, or maybe flattered me, or maybe it was something else. I'd always hungered to be known, hungered for someone to be interested enough to try to figure me out. Perhaps the need arose from believing that my mother never cared.

Whatever it was, Jagwire's words hit a sensitive spot and sparked a romance that continued for months. It wasn't so much what he said, but an emptiness he'd accidentally filled. Jagwire happened to say something that plugged right into the hardware of my brain.

Though some may regard an Internet romance as existing only in one's mind and not in reality, the emotional part is certainly real for the participants. To cyber citizens, what happens online is a very real part of their lives. And discounting sleep, a growing number of us spend an equal or greater amount of time online than off.

Jagwire said the right words to spark my interest and I ran off with him to frolic in his Cave of the Falling Waters. Though I didn't usually reveal my character's name to people I met in the Sex Room as a guest, I told him who I was and other true facts about myself. I'd been impressed by the intelligence that came through his words as conspicuously as something in html encased in <BLINK> </BLINK>. If you're a smart person, it's apparent in MOO dialogue; if you're a jerk, that's obvious, too. Jagwire was artistic, creative, and intelligent—traits I found irresistible in VR and RL. His creativity showed in the lines of description he gave his MOO jungle and in the stalking panthers that padded through every three minutes as part of a program.

We had MOO sex in his pond and snuggled afterward on a lily pad. I liked him. I must have attracted him as well, for we were soon a MOO couple, exchanging email several times a day and meeting every night. We also had forbidden rendezvous during the day. As a graphics designer, he spent his office hours on a computer and sometimes he snuck open an extra window to play with me on Anjuna Beach, a virtual space I'd created on World MOO where I was still anonymous. No one but Jagwire knew that I was "Patpong" on Sprawl and on Lambda but "Anjuna" on World MOO.

I wrapped my arms around Jagwire's neck and rested my chin on his shoulder, tilting my head against his as we both looked at his computer screen. I kissed his neck—or rather I typed :kisses your neck, which appeared on his screen as *Anjuna kisses your neck*. With me in New York and Jagwire in California, we'd never met in RL. The

":" (called the "emote" command) is used to denote actions. Next, I typed *:hugs you tighter*, which appeared to him as *Anjuna hugs you tighter*. He answered with *Jagwire kisses you passionately.*

For several months Jagwire was my VR boyfriend. We rushed home after work to be together every evening. We met either in his jungle on Lambda MOO or on my Anjuna Beach on World MOO. We'd chat about the day's events and about anything new in our lives. Then we'd have MOO sex, tearing off each other's clothes until all that were left were our "naked messages," his with a massive erection and mine with soft pubic hair and firm perky breasts.

The final piece of "clothing" I had to *strip* from him was called *"last hint of shame,"* a legacy from his strict religious upbringing, testimony to how we re-create our psyche to the point of incarnating unconscious imprints.

One day I decided to show him Patpong Road. *See Chiba City Limits?* I asked him. *From there, go north three blocks and turn west onto Micro Avenue.*

Sprawl MOO is connected to the Web to form a WOO (Web plus MOO), created by the Sprawl God "wizrocker," a.k.a. Sam Latt Epstein. With WOO every MOO object has a .property that can be written in html and accessed by a netbrowser.

WOO Transaction Protocol (WTP) is an internet communications protocol designed to integrate two well known internet services: World Wide Web (WWW) and Multi User Object Oriented Environments (MOO) creating WOO. WTP provides a means for MOO servers to serve HTML documents to WWW clients. . . . (Epstein, electronic document)

Okay, I'm at Patpong Road, Jagwire said, or rather typed, into one of the windows on his screen, the window we shared on World MOO. Our cyber bodies lay together in a hammock on Anjuna Beach. Outside the window, he was on the Web with Netscape. I'd told him to WOO to Sprawl MOO, where I'd just linked some pictures taken of me and a few of the prostitutes I knew in Thailand.

You're on Patpong Road? I typed to Jagwire. *Now click on the highlighted text that says picture of Patpong on Patpong Road.*

I got it, he said. *You with your arms around a Thai guy.* He added a ":("—the online representation of a sad face—to express his jealousy at seeing me with another man. Though Echo frowned at the use of emoticons like the smiley and the frowny, I tolerated the fact that denizens of other virtual spaces still used them.

I answered *:smiles.* and then *:kisses you deeply for you are the only meaningful man in her life.*

Jagwire closed Netscape and brought forward the Anjuna Beach window so he could give me his undivided attention. He took me in his arms and pushed his body against mine as we entangled in the hammock. He pressed his crotch to me and caressed my legs with his hand. His erection grew and I arched my back against him, running my fingers through his hair as our tongues met. Periodically, an ambience message appeared, like a fly buzzing, a breeze in the trees.

He typed *Strip dress from Anjuna*, and because I'd

entered the permission command that allowed him to do that, the screen announced *Jagwire removes Anjuna's yellow sundress.*

After he typed *strip bra from Anjuna*, and *strip panties from Anjuna*, I was down to my "naked message." I removed his clothing, too, including the *last hint of shame.* Encouragingly, I wrote *:melts in your arms.—: opens her legs for you in mad passion.—:moans as you enter her.*

Anyone on the MOO who chose to @look at us during those moments would read our "naked messages." Anyone doing a @who would see our names and location—two people in a locked room, stripped to their naked messages—and would know exactly what we were doing. MOO sex.

Jagwire was expert at it. It could be distracting if your partner suddenly had you facing up when you envisioned down, or was in back of you when you'd just gestured to the front. MOO actions required an imagination adept at maintaining the vision of who was where in relation to whom, the location of all the legs and arms, and all the changes in position. Jarring, mismatched dialogue ruined the mood. A leg in the air when you pictured it on the ground broke the scenario, reminding you that your hands were on a room-temperatured keyboard and not a hot-blooded man.

But Jagwire's depictions were congruent. When I twisted this way, his body adjusted. Our hips met rhythmically in sexual synchronization. We searched each other's emotes for clues to the onset of orgasm and cried out in unison.

Jagwire says, "Ooooooooooooooooooooooooooooo-o."

Anjuna says, "AAAAAAAAAAAAAAAAAAAAA-AAAAAAAA."

Jagwire says, "I love you, Cleo."

Anjuna mmmmms, "I love you, too."

Virtual climax over, we kissed and lay quietly in the hammock, Jagwire hugging me tightly.

I gotta go, I typed eventually. *But I hate always being the one to rush off.*

I understand, he typed back. *I'm sorry for keeping you up late, so you're tired the next day.* With the difference between our RL homes, my bedtime was his dinnertime. *Good night, sweetheart,* he said.

A parrot I'd programmed to respond to certain words, one of which was "sweetheart," squawked, *Sweetheart. Sweetheart. Jagwire's got a sweetheart.*

With a final *:kisses you goodbye,* I @quit the MOO and shut down the computer.

3. Sex at the Palace

▶ In November 1995, I discovered the Palace, a graphical virtual space, a mansion of twenty-nine rooms where members create their own "avatars" (or "avs"), images to represent themselves—a scanned photo or a cartoon drawing. Unlike the text-only MOO, where you use your imagination to see yourself in a described room, the Palace presents an eye-popping colored picture of your physical location. If I see a chair, I can place my avatar in it. If I want a beer, I double-click the beer glass in my "prop bag" and a beer appears in my hand.

I took six rolls of pictures so I could have an avatar to express various moods—one with my hand waving in greeting, a laughing one, a sad one, an angry one, and an attentive one. I made two avs of me in bathing suits for use in the Palace pool or on the Palace beach. I had a dancing avatar and one sleeping with a BRB (Be Right Back) sign, meaning I was away from the keyboard.

I knew from the start that this make-your-own-av feature also allowed people to scan in porn pictures, which might one day be problematic. A few months later this suspicion proved true.

The Palace uses a text-to-speech program so that users can hear what people type as well as see it in a cartoon speech balloon on the screen. After a year and a half as a MOO addict, I didn't think twice about ditching the MOO for the Palace. Though I'd joined while the Palace was still in its testing phase, I felt immediately: "This is it!" Since then, it has had regular upgrades, each one making it more versatile, each fulfilling a little more the potential that I had initially sensed. The Palace is the baby of Jim Bumgardner, conceptualized through years of visualization. At the sight of it, this anthropologist, who's traveled the world and who'd lived six years in cyberspace, felt awestruck.

Even without the text-to-speech application, the Palace comes with sounds that anyone can make. The ")kiss" produces a kissing noise and the ")wind" and ")wet1" allow for two varieties of farts. People can make two kinds of laughter—the ")teehee" for a giggle or the ")guffaw." They can also ")ow" and ")amen."

Only members can wear personal avatars. Guests are restricted to round green faces, but they can activate the noises, and seem particularly fond of the farts.

I love to program things and have spent marathon hours inside the MOO "editor," the place to fix and fine-tune creations. The Palace also fulfills that urge to program (or write "scripts," as it's called there), though without the intricacies available in MUDs and MOOs. I've no doubt it will become more flexible as Jim tailors his newly born phenomenon to meet our virtual-citizenship needs.

People from chat-only places, such as IRC (Internet

Relay Chat), are finding a home on the Palace, too. However, those of us with roots in the fantasy realms find their inclination to yell, "Age? Sex? Location?" a tad annoying.

The main Palace gets hundreds of people logged in at a time, with thousands of guests visiting daily. Members are making their own Palaces, and soon these will be crowded, too, as people spread out to find their niche. When you register, you get the software to be a Palace server. My Palace site was called Goa. I did consider how innovative a brothel might be, but by then I couldn't face the thought of one more prostitute.

To make their own sites, people can use the original mansion rooms or delete them and draw their own. Palace sites have opened all over—France, Brazil, Trinidad, Japan. Some have themes—a sports Palace, a gay and lesbian Palace, quite a few sex Palaces.

I still checked in daily to the MOOs, though I had exchanged my MOO time for the Palace. I maintain characters on thirteen of them but only talk to a handful of old friends, and if they aren't on, I "idle" (logged in, but without interaction). After I became Web master at my job, with a PPP connection on my office computer, I'd leave some MOO windows open in the background while I worked. If StarDancer or Jagwire or Quinn paged, I could answer. Unfortunately, the Palace, with its bright colors and loud voices, is not something one can do surreptitiously while at work.

I was so wowed by the potential of Palace technology that early in 1996, when I was asked to become a Palace wizard, I accepted the unpaid job, though I knew the commitment it entailed. I felt honored to join in the development of the new VR. Though I'd turned down several offers to wiz a MOO, the Palace was something I believed in, and I wanted to be a part of its inception no matter how much time and effort it took.

According to cyberspace hierarchy, a "wizard" is someone who has special powers and who performs certain duties. Gods have the highest powers and are usually the owners or creators of the space. System operators (sys ops) reign over one area or perhaps a board. CompuServe is divided into forums, each moderated by a sys op (also called a section leader). Whatever the context, these people have control over others. Many put in long, arduous hours for no pay, with the awe and respect of their flocks their only reward.

I know the joys and the potentials for abuse that come with power. As a wizard on the Palace, I can gag, kill, and site-ban. Once I overcame the fear of being disliked, I reveled in pinning someone to a corner with graphic chains. My mother taught me the feminine art of covert criticism—the sigh, the stinging joke, sarcasm—but to be a wizard I had to say outright: *That behavior is not allowed here*, which led to *I don't allow that behavior here and I don't care if it's not written in a rule book. It bothers* me.

Being a wizard is a course in assertiveness training. If a snerty guest annoys a member, I'll warn him a few times, then *pow*, I'll execute. The guest will vanish off the screen. I can set the death penalty from zero minutes, meaning they could log right back on, to months, as I saw fit. Killing a miscreant feels so good, I'd be disappointed if a night went by without at least one slaughter.

What attracts me to a persona on the Palace? On the MOO, I often wondered why I found one character appealing while others bored me. Jagwire's perception of me and Quinn's brilliant programming set off something in me. Other net crushes are harder to explain. What did Peter write in email that sparked my interest? On the Palace, with its graphics, I'm drawn to furry creatures. I've always loved fur but never realized my attraction to it until I noted how I'm irresistibly impelled toward furry avatars. I see a tiger and rush to its side. I don a cat avatar, which allows me to rub up against the tiger and utter *meow*. Often the tiger answers with *purr*. I *purr* back. Nice flirtation.

This sometimes extends into a sexual interest toward the man behind the picture. Fortunately, people change avatars frequently on the Palace, and there's no bigger disappointment than seeing a sexy tiger turn into Bart Simpson. If not for that, I'd be in love with a half a dozen guys and would never get out of the Palace bedrooms.

One man I met wore an avatar of a handsome cutie pie in a cutaway T-shirt. I flirted with him outrageously. I'd move my avatar so it looked like I was sitting on his lap. When he entered a room, I greeted him with my ")kiss" script, and when I wore my elephant avatar, which had three different trunk positions, I used the trunk shamelessly to caress his face and even his crotch. One day, he wore a picture of an ugly fat man. I laughed.

This is my real photo, he said. What a letdown. Afterward I felt obliged to continue the flirtations so as not to not hurt his feelings, but the thrill was gone.

The hundreds of tennis-ball-looking male guests who log on the Palace looking for women don't stand a chance next to the hunky avatars that members wear. I guess they end up pairing off into the bedrooms with other guests. Guests can appear female by wearing a pink wig prop, a blond ponytail, long eyelashes, or a bikini top. I know a guy who takes a break from his office job by going on as a female guest and luring male guests into the Honeymoon Suite. It's amazing to see the unsuspecting new guest trail after a pink-wigged green face as if she were Marilyn Monroe. The main Palace has four bedrooms that can be locked. For a romantic setting, it's possible to dim the lights in the room, making the background go dark but still visible.

How to have cyber sex on the Palace? After the MOO, this presented a challenge. What could I do when the Palace didn't have a way to emote actions? MOO sex occurs mostly with actions, not by speech. *Cleo puts her arms around your neck and kisses you passionately.* I didn't know how to produce that image in a speech balloon. On the other hand, the graphic capabilities piqued my interest. I could use photos to depict sex acts, though I had no intention of using nudes of myself.

I wanted to experience sex on the Palace so I asked Tomato to try it with me. We were no longer cyber lovers, just friends, but we'd fucked so much in the past, he seemed perfect for the experiment. In preparation, I scanned porn pictures to represent what we were doing.

I scanned ten pictures and converted them to GIFs and arranged to meet Tomato at his Palace so I wouldn't be interrupted by wizard duties. His site was a lovely marble hall on a grassy hill descending to a sea.

Nice background GIF, I commented, *but this marble may be a bit hard to lie on. Don'tcha have a pillow?*

You're right. I need to add a bed.

So, how do we do this? I asked, a Palace virgin.

I don't know.

Though we'd had sex every day for months the year before, we were lost over how to do it in this medium.

He put on a nude. *Oo oo*, I responded with enthusiasm, though I'd seen it before when he visited my Goa hippie-beach Palace. I changed into an avatar of a brunette lying sideways, wearing only a blouse opened to reveal her breasts and exposing her naked lower half. I hoped the patch of pubic hair would inspire him.

He didn't comment. *How do you like this one?* he asked as he changed into a male wearing a mask and sporting a long erection.

The standard Palace avatar is a forty-four-by-forty-four-pixel box, but members can combine boxes to make larger ones. His nude was nine boxes big, while mine was only one.

Yum, I responded, though I felt too small to fit with his picture, and my vision of intimacy was knocked out of kilter. He didn't seem to be getting aroused either. On the MOO a simple: *Cleo runs her fingers up your arm* would have been enough to have him answer: *Tomato's cock grows hard and he pulls you toward him.*

I felt unsexy.

I changed into the most erotic photo I had—a woman facing down, eyes closed, sucking on a penis that was halfway in her mouth. But I felt like a failure. Our positions didn't match. His nine boxes represented a man standing up with an erection pointing to the left, and I was a one-box little face aiming down over a penis. Totally mismatched.

On the MOO, we'd been able to adjust our positions so what we typed and envisioned was congruent. We weren't accomplishing that with the graphics.

I had another blow-job avatar, this one going left to right instead of up and down, and I switched to it. Unfortunately, Tomato was on my right with his erection pointed left, and my avatar had the face pointing left and the penis going right. So that didn't match either.

This isn't working well, he noted.

Yeah, how do we do this? We're both creative, sexual, and artistic—we should be able to work this out.

He changed to a close-up of a penis entering a shaved vagina.

Oh yes, do that to me, I said. *I want you in me.*

I had an intercourse photo, too, though mine was smaller and showed the bodies instead of just the genitals. Again it struck me that we weren't on the same wavelength. He was on one side of the screen and I was on the other. When I moved my icon on top of his, he noted, *Now it looks like four people in an orgy.*

There must be a way to do this, I said, feeling frustrated. I'd gotten aroused preparing for the encounter, poring through porn magazines looking for the poses that would represent the sex acts we were doing. That had been a turn-on. I had chosen the pictures I wanted to engage in mentally, but our sex acts weren't connecting. The images still didn't fit, and we still had no way to emote actions.

Tomato changed back into the masked man with an erection. I put on a bent-over, naked-butt shot. Since cyber sex uses language to describe the sex acts you imagine performing, the mechanics of arousal involve sexual descriptions and saying sexy things. I thought I'd try "saying" what we used to accomplish by "emoting" on the MOO. Whereas on the MOO I could have typed, *Cleo moves her naked ass against your cock*, on the Palace, the best I could do was have a speech balloon coming from the naked ass saying, *Come to me with your throbbing dick*.

I moved the butt photo up against his erection photo and it almost looked like it fit, but now what? There was no way to make actions, you could only talk. *I'm so hot for you*, I said, *I want you in me*.

By this time, though, he seemed to have given up on our project and asked. *How do you like my ocean? I'm going to draw another room with a beach.*

With this clue that his mind was no longer on sex, I changed back to the avatar of the reclining female. I answered him on the subject of Paint programs while contemplating how to get him back to the task at hand. With a mouse click, I moved my avatar from the marble floor to the grass below and noted, *It's nice and soft here on the grass*. I switched to an avatar of a female with her legs spread, fingering her vagina. *I'm so hot I can't stop touching myself.*

I realized he had no pictures that would fit with what I looked like. We regressed to hot-chatting and got it over quickly. Though I ended with an orgasm, I was displeased and somehow unsatisfied and logged off soon after. This reinforces the notion that it's possible to have an online sexual interaction that leads to orgasm but leaves you feeling unsatisfied and a virtual sexual interaction that ends with only a cyber orgasm that, nevertheless, leaves you deeply satiated.

After spending some time on the Palace, a few characters caught my attention. Who knows why? Sometimes I can figure out part of the reason I'm attracted to an RL guy. Perhaps he fits my image of "cute." Perhaps he taps into a memory of someone else, like Jeremy Berg did at Echo school. Perhaps he says something that hits the right button. If I meet someone I like at an RL party, I might call my friend the next day and say, "I met a cute guy last night. He's smart and funny and sexy." In truth, I probably don't have a clue as to why that particular guy caught my fancy. Likewise, the strangest things turn me off.

This happens online, too. A man named Storm Shadow had a sexy avatar of a desert-type hunk with a veiled face—Lawrence of Arabia style. He caught my interest and we whispered suggestively to each other. Then his spelling got on my nerves.

At first his typos were just distracting. Everyone

makes typos. It's expected. When someone corrects something they spelled wrong, I answer, *I knew what you meant. I speak typo fluently.* But Storm Shadow made too many and they were odd. *Your spelling is strange*, I couldn't help telling him.

Must be my southern accent, he answered, which didn't explain sentences like: *Theirs a lot of peple in herre tonit.* Grammatical mistakes are the norm, too. The *frequency* of their occurrence differentiates an error from a mark of illiteracy. Within minutes, I stopped seeing Storm Shadow as a sexy hunk and started picturing him as an idiot, uneducated, disheveled, lazy, and so lacking in concern for others that he didn't care if he confused them with sentences that needed to be deciphered by a professional cryptographer.

Flirting is fun. I love to flirt with cute male avatars. I turn into a chimpanzee when I spot a chimpanzee. I knuckle-walk close to it. Is this a species connection? An evolutionary throwback? A chimpanzee can only produce offspring with another chimpanzee. Perhaps that coding still exists in the most ancient and primitive part of our brain.

One night I wore a moose avatar. Feu des Astres, a regular at the Palace who had worn enough hunky pictures to arouse my hormones, was alone with me in the room. He, too, donned the moose, and after flipping mine horizontally so that we faced each other, I put myself, moose nose to moose nose, up against him.

Feu des Astres said, *Smooch*.

I answered, *Smooch*, and made the Palace kissing noise. And so went another flirting session. It wasn't much. I soon had to leave on wizard business. But it was as stimulating as an RL flirtation at a party. It makes your blood pump faster, and a smile tugs at your lips. Flirting is as enticing online as off. Another time, I went to Feu des Astres's Palace site. We wore bathing suits and stood close together in his beachside parlor. We were the only two on his site. Being alone with someone on his Palace is like being alone with a guy in his apartment—I wouldn't be there if I didn't want to be. My interest in Feu increased that night. Where we were and what we wore connoted intimacy. If I wanted to break the spell, I could have changed into the duck avatar I sometimes wore in the swimming pool on the main Palace. A goofy cartoon duck is sure to dissipate a seductive atmosphere.

While some attractions happen right away, others develop over time. First, nothing; then a curiosity; then infatuation. I called Feu des Astres "Fur" because my text-to-speech application says "Fia" instead of Feu, and "fur" is sort of close to the French pronunciation of feu. I'd known Fur months before becoming attracted to him. Maybe my interest in him arose from his creativity. He was known for making beautiful avatars for women and he made me some, too, without my asking. He took the modeling photos on my homepage and turned them into nine-box avatars. Other guys have given me avatars, and though I appreciated the gifts, they never warmed me sexually. Gift giving is a courtship ritual and the only gifts you can give on the Palace are avatars and scripts. Placing flowers or candy near someone is a similar gesture but a "cheaper" effort.

One night, Fur and I entered a locked bedroom so he could give me another avatar he'd made me. I donned a naked cartoon avatar and lay on the bed. Fur wore his sexy-man-in-a-bathing-suit avatar. *Oooo*, I responded. *Does that suit come off?*

Not on the main Palace, he answered.

Aw. I put on an even sexier cartoon, a naked woman on hands and knees, with a hint of genitals displayed. Fur donned a sexier avatar, too. Soon I was wearing some of the porn I'd made for the sex with Tomato. Fur changed to a naked seated male with legs open. I had to unselect the option "show names" because Fur's name was covering the most interesting part. I noted that he'd broken his rule about not wearing nudes on the main Palace. We weren't talking sexy, though. *Oh, I want that av*, I said. *Can I have it?*

Sure, he answered. I used the wizard command "clone" and changed my avatar to a copy of his. We became two naked men on the bed. I placed mine directly behind his so it looked like he was sitting between my legs. *I've always wanted to be a gay male*, I said, adding a "*)teehee.*"

I went through all my porn and he showed me his collection of naked female avatars. He sometimes used a female name, and not wanting to blow his cover, I was careful not to call him Fur when he entered Harry's Bar in his alternate character.

Though we didn't get into sex talk that night, and I

soon left on wizard patrol, my interest in Fur increased a notch more.

He'd long been on my flirt list. I had dozens of guys on the list, but now Fur moved into the "possible sex partner" category, where there was only one other name— Mr. Hyde, whom I'd seen in video on CUseeme and whose long blond hair had triggered a "boyfriend material" reaction.

Miss Tina's Palace, called the Dungeon, is my favorite Palace to go to when I want to get away from TPI (The Palace Inc.) Palaces and my duties there. When someone creates their own site, they can use whatever background photo they want. Miss Tina has a meadow where I've lolled naked in cartoon avatars. On Tina's Palace, anything goes and I dare to be as lewd as I want. When I want to relax and hang out, it's to Tina's I go.

Miss Tina is a lively seductress, out to cyber-fuck every appealing male and female member. Her site has rooms with GIFs of close-up orgy porn and a variety of bedrooms.

One night, at the front gate on Main (what we call the main TPI Palace), Miss Tina whispered, *You're invited, too.*

To what? I whispered back. When many people are in one room, I lose track of what's said, and the Palace Gate, the log-in room, rarely has fewer than ten.

Party at my site, she told me. *Now*.

It was late, near the time I usually log off, but I decided to drop by for a minute. Four others were on Tina's Palace, in the Meadow, which was a GIF of grass under a willow tree.

I spotted Fur leaning against the tree. *Hey, Fur, can I wear the naked guy you gave me?*

Sure. When I became the male, a member named Dreamy donned a picture of a seated female bending forward. She moved it in front of my penis. We all laughed. Fur donned a naked man that had one leg raised, blocking his genitals. I changed to a naked female cartoon, lying sideways, and placed it to look like my head was in Fur's lap.

Tina whispered, *Are you fucking Feu?*

Not yet, I answered. *But I'd like to. Have you?*

No, but I will.

Though it was my bedtime, I stayed. The Meadow was cozy and I felt relaxed and content lolling with Fur.

Two people logged off, leaving just the three of us. Fur had given me a standing nude female that fit nicely with a standing nude male he had. We put them on and it looked like we were embracing. After a few seconds of silence I said, *Tina, come join us.*

She moved in. Tina started by saying, *Moving my hand between Cleo's legs.* Since I knew Tina was the Palace sex goddess, I understood that this was the way to have Palace sex, even though it seemed strange coming from speech balloons. I wrote: *Moving closer to Fur and putting my arms around his waist and around Tina, drawing her closer.*

Tina changed the room GIF from a meadow to a close-up of a woman holding an erect penis while licking another woman's clit.

And so began our threeway. By now I was hot for Fur and I liked Tina, too. I cringed when Tina said, *Shoving my fist up Cleo's cunt,* but . . . well, that was Tina's way. When Tina said, *I'm putting a dildo in me in RL,* I went for my vibrator and plugged it in. I held it against me by crossing my legs. Since there were three of us, I had extra time between contributing lines of dialogue. I was so turned on by kissing Fur and having his virtual cock in me that I achieved orgasm. I could tell by his deep tongue kissing and slow caresses on my breast that Fur was the type to spend five hours in a net-sex session, though. Since it was late and I was RL sexually satisfied, I left.

The next day I tried to get on Fur's Palace but couldn't. I looked for him on Main. Hours later he showed up. I was happy to see him. I was willing to go to his site for a private session, though I wasn't feeling particularly horny. I just wanted to be with him.

I've been trying to get on your site, I told him, *but it says Connection Refused.*

It's up, Fur answered.

I immediately disconnected and tried again but still couldn't get on.

Back on Main, I told him, *It won't let me in.*

Well, I'm here, so you know it's up, he said, which I found a bit snotty. I'd hoped he'd sound glad to see me. *Why did you disappear so fast last night?* he asked.

Got dumped by my internet service provider, I lied. *What happened after I left?*

We continued.

I'm jealous, I whispered, not really jealous but fishing for a compliment or some nice words about how he'd missed me. None came.

I tried again to get on his site but couldn't. *Still no*

good, I told him, once more back on Main. *Do you have a dynamic IP?* A dynamic IP is one that changes the address every time you log on.

Yes. He gave me the number of his current one.

Well gee! Now you tell me? No wonder I couldn't get on if I was trying an old number. By this time I was sad and annoyed that he wasn't gushing over my presence. *But I'm not trying again,* I said, huffing, RL emotions blending with VR events. *I don't want to go anymore.*

Just as well, he said. *I'm at work, so we couldn't start anything.*

I logged off soon after, miffed that he wasn't expressing affection. I felt rejected. I didn't really want a relationship with Fur, but I did want to play some more. His lack of interest hurt my feelings. My emotional reactions were real, though the VR situation was cloudy and ambiguous.

In 1996, when I made a business trip to Bangkok, I got my old friend Richard, whom I knew from Goa, and his friend Jamie hooked on the Palace. Needing an Internet fix, I ran often to Richard's house to log in and ease my Internet withdrawal symptoms. When Jamie saw the Palace, he became addicted right away. Jamie ran a Bangkok bbs called Sala Thai, and when he became a Palace addict, Sala Thai lost some of his attention.

A few weeks after I returned to New York, Miss Tina lured Jamie to her Palace. In the same way that you can multi-MOO, you can multi-Palace—be on more than one Palace at a time.

When I found Jamie in Harry's Bar on Main, he told me *Come to Tina's.* In an instant I was there.

Tina! Tina! Haha, you've got Jamie in your clutches.

I suspected Jamie wasn't acquainted with cyber sex, mostly because the connection from Thailand was slow, irregular, and expensive, but also because he was happily married. I didn't want to be the one to initiate him into it for several reasons. Not only did I know his wife, but Jamie was a friend, which made it awkward. I couldn't resist showing off the Palace's potential, though. I donned a naked avatar.

Jamie exclaimed, *Wow!*

Tina was quick to join the fun and also got naked. She used a picture of a woman with her legs spread. *"Oh wow,"* said Jamie. I *)teeheed*.

Tina and I ran through our wardrobe of nudies. Jamie *Ohhed* when Tina put on a photo of a female spearing herself with a dildo. I animated a face with a protruding tongue that flicked up and down as if licking a dick.

Jamie, look what I can do! Isn't this animation great?

Jamie didn't have a nude and remained dressed in a suit and hat, looking like a Mormon in a whorehouse.

Jamie, hon, you gotta get those pants off, said Tina.

Then Tina gave me an avatar to wear. It showed a naked woman kneeling, but half of her breast was missing. I was about to remark on it when Tina put on the other half of the picture—another naked kneeling woman. When she placed her avatar next to mine, the two women were embracing, the aforementioned breast not missing but squashed against the other woman's body. I)teeheed again.

Tina and I moved so that Jamie was squeezed between us in a sandwich. Tina and I had done a threesome before, with Fur, but I didn't feel comfortable doing one with Jamie.

When the situation became too serious and sensual, I said, *Gotta go!* and disconnected.

Jules has been having computer sex via the Intranet and the Internet for twenty-three years. After a long time in AOL chat rooms, he now restricts himself to Palace sex. For him, the specialty of the Palace is its voice capabilities. He can hear what his partner is saying she's doing to him. He uses a standard nude avatar for his sex acts; the idea of having an assortment of porn pictures never interested him.

His primary reason for starting his own Palace was to have a private place to meet his cyber lover. They were involved in a love affair that had lasted four months. They met once in person, but could not continue an RL courtship because they lived in different states and couldn't afford continual meetings in person. At the moment Jules is involved in an RL relationship and is living with a woman. He says he generally doesn't have cyber sex when involved in an RL relationship, but that occasionally an innocent friendly Palace chat may get sexual.

During his fifteen months on the Palace, he's had seven sexual partners. He's been attracted to many online women but doesn't usually pursue them. His cyber-sex experiences have not affected his RL sex acts in any way. He says he doesn't get jealous and obsessive in RL or in VR.

"Do you have orgasms with cyber sex?" I asked.

"Yes! But mental ones."

4. CUseedick

A black-and-white computer video camera costs ninety-nine dollars. With it, and the free software that is available on the net, people can communicate by real-time video. As a long-time cyber citizen, I was not surprised to find that a major use of video-conferencing was sex.

After my first attempt to connect to a popular CU-seeme "reflector," where you can see up to eight other people, I started calling it CUseedick. When I disconnected from the reflector, someone followed me and flashed a close-up video of his naked hard-on.

On my third try at CUseedick, I realized the medium could, indeed, be arousing. Some CU guys just wanted me to watch them jerk off, and that seemed like fun. They said I could turn my "send-video" off so that I could watch while remaining unseen. You can't flash nudity on public university reflectors, so these conversations happened after I disconnected from a site and before quitting CU-seeme. Someone would follow me to my IP address and have me in a one-on-one.

For fun I agreed to go along. I kept my video turned on, though, thinking I'd be contributing by showing my

> Hi! Welcome to Videodate, for live interactive CUseeme Sex Dates with sexy models from Holland!
>
> Here you can find out:
>
> * What Videodate is, how it came about, and what it has to offer.
>
> * What you need to "connect now" and "pay later," and how to get it:
>
> — CUseeme, the (free) videoconferencing software.
>
> — A First Virtual account, to pay securely, using your credit card.
>
> * What it looks like when you're actually connected.
>
> * What WE look like.
>
> Just DO it: """" Connect NOW and pay later! """"
> (http://www.exe.nl/)

face looking interested. I shocked myself the first time I got so aroused by what I was witnessing that I joined in and flashed a few seconds of my bush.

The guy I flashed had named himself "X." Once, after checking a few reflectors but not finding anyone attractive, I was about to quit when someone named "X Dressed" clicked onto my screen. Because of my encounter with X, I didn't realize at first what X Dressed meant or that he was a different person. All I saw in the video was the guy's lower half sitting at his computer. Finally I realized he was wearing a slip over a garter belt with black stockings—a cross-dresser!

Wanna watch me fuck myself with a dildo? he asked.

Hey, now that could be entertaining. *Sure*, I answered. After a blur of movement too quick for the camera to capture, I saw him bent over, butt naked in his garter belt. He inserted a dildo in his ass. Though his hand movements made the video jumpy, looking like something seen in strobe lighting, I could see the dildo go deep inside and then be pulled almost out. After a few minutes he turned around so I could watch him ejaculate.

On someone's homepage called "CU-Sleazy," the person put some screen captures of people he'd seen, including one of a woman lifting her top and showing off her naked breasts with the caption:

> It's hard for me to say what I like best about CU-seeme.
>
> Could it be the chance to see the interesting gestures and facial expressions that the images provide? Or is it the attraction of peering into folks' dens and admiring their interesting head-wear? Nope, I think the real reason I like CUseeme is . . . the cheap thrill from seeing a stranger's hooters in 16 shades of gray. http://www.btf.com/cuseeme/

On Echo, I'd found a list of reflector sites, but they were mostly at universities and were often filled to capacity and not accepting callers. I learned that addresses of cool refs (reflectors) were guarded, cherished secrets.

Because of the limited number of people allowed on at a time, regulars didn't tell strangers the addresses of their favorite sites. After the first experience with X, where I got so involved that I flashed a stranger, the possibilities of what I could do and see with video conferencing overran my imagination and I was eager to try out this new toy. Where to find the right guy? How to find a good ref?

I started hanging out on channel #cuseeme on IRC to meet people, hoping they'd give me the hot ref numbers. First, I had to convince someone I was female. Often this meant going one-on-one with them by video. IRC also has a channel #cuseemesexy, which was loaded with guys panting to C-me. But I didn't want to jump into a one-on-one without seeing the person first, and since IRC is text only, I never knew what the name "Handsome Dude" really represented. I preferred meeting them on a public ref, where there'd be several people. That way, it wouldn't seem like such an insult if I thought "bleh" at the sight of the guy and declined to join him in a private session. By this time I'd learned how to prevent people following from me from a ref and popping onto my screen uninvited. I unchecked the "accept all callers" in the software option so that I'd get a message that so-and-so wanted to connect, and I could accept or refuse.

It's not easy to get out of a cyber-sex encounter that isn't working. After a while on CompuServe's CB, when I found myself faking an orgasm in order to log off gracefully, I decided I'd had enough of that. By the time I frequented the Sex Room on Lambda MOO as an anonymous guest, I found it simpler to escape. I just disconnected without an excuse. Occasionally, I felt a twinge of guilt about leaving a guy in the lurch alone in a bedroom, but why stay once it's obvious that the sex isn't working? People have disconnected on me, too—sometimes due to uncontrollable factors, like a server going down or someone walking in the room. You learn not to take it too personally.

When you're face-to-face with someone on video, though, it's harder to disengage. In my second week of CUseeme-ing, I did it twice. The encounters just weren't exciting. Worse, they were downright tedious.

I felt bad the first time. I had a cute young guy on the screen. He told me his name and where he lived. We smiled at each other and laughed at a few jokes. Then he took off his clothes and positioned the camera so I'd see his cock. He stroked it to make it erect. I lifted the top of my shirt so he could see my breasts. I rolled a nipple in my fingers. His hand moved his cock so it aimed straight up and then came down so its slit pointed right at the camera.

I wasn't aroused. For some reason, the scene just didn't turn me on. I was bored and suspected he might take an hour to finish. I groaned at the thought. I didn't want to proceed further. What to do? I sat through another minute before deciding I couldn't stand another second— the same hand movement; the same penis eye glaring at the camera lens. I edged my hand slowly toward the mouse while smiling sweetly at the camera. Still smiling, with an interested look on my face, I covertly pulled down the menu and chose the option "disconnect." What a heartless bitch I was. How could I ever face that guy again? I'd have to stay off the ref where we met.

I felt so bad that the next day I posted about it in the Internet Conference on Echo. After it happened a second time I realized I had to be more selective. I decided that before committing myself, I had to be sure I'd follow through to conclusion. I wanted to delve into the depths of CUseeme sex but only with someone I really wanted. And I knew just the person! Mars! A Lambda character I'd long lusted over.

I paged Mars on Lambda MOO and told him I had a quickcam. *Do you CU?* I asked. *I have a camera*, he answered, *but I don't get much opportunity to use it*. He gave me a url for where he had uploaded on the Web some nude photos of himself, though. I rushed to take a look.

Wow! What a treat to see his lovely erection. I wondered if sharing the photos with me was an invitation for CU sex. After a few flirting MOO messages, we planned to try it together. I thrilled to hear the excitement when he paged, *HUBBA HUBBA*.

The night of our date, the net was slow. The lag was bad all along the eastern seaboard and Echo had posted that Alternet and UUnet, the main routers for the area, were doing upgrades.

So during the first few moments when I had Mars's beautiful face, live on my screen, I noted, *The net is slow today*. He complained of getting bad reception. One-on-one video is usually pretty good, and if you move slowly you can get the appearance of video action even in the presence of lag.

I was more than ready for Mars, though I sensed his annoyance at the lag. When he asked me for confirmation of my intentions, I eagerly pulled down my nightgown, in a slow stripper style.

I saw him smile. A kaleidoscope effect on my screen indicated fast motion, and my heart skipped a beat as I thought I could make out the tip of his erect penis. And then . . . disconnected!

Had he disconnected on purpose because he wasn't into it? He didn't want to have CU sex with me? The lag made it not worth it?

I tried twice to reconnect to his site. No response. After the time I'd turned off the "accept all callers," I knew that the person being called received a "ring" message with the option to accept the connection or not. I was so crushed by the thought that Mars had deliberately disconnected on me and was refusing my calls that I couldn't bring myself to log back onto the MOO to page him.

The next day, I logged on the MOO and found out that he'd been disconnected, too. He'd sent me urgent pages: *How could you leave me when I was burning for you?*

Unfortunately, Mars could only log on from his office. Since his boss would surely frown if he caught Mars jerking off in a room with three other employees, he had to be alone there to do it. He paged, *I want you so badly!* which sent tingles through my body. But every night when I was ready, he had people working beside him.

One thing I noticed from gender bending on the MOO is the conditioning society forces on us to make us into girls or boys. To be convincing as a female (where insiders know that half the women are really men) I giggle and blush and avoid being too aggressive. On the other hand, when I log on as a male, I don't giggle and I'm demanding, suggestive, and bold. As a male, I can more easily touch my body parts and those of other people and speak in cruder language. I'm allowed to be more openly sexual.

I'd noted in my research on gender relations that "good girls" are not supposed to sexual. They're only allowed to enjoy it when in love. To otherwise express desire is forbidden.

Though polygamy has been officially declared illegal in Thailand, Thai men still marry one women after another without legal sanction. Men have "major" wives and "minor" wives, and there's a nighttime soap opera called the *Mia Noi*, which means the "Minor Wife." A Thai woman, on the other hand, is considered "bad" for having more than one lover and there is no such thing as a "minor husband."

In 1991, I presented a paper at a conference on gender and industrialization in Asia and ended up arguing with an economics professor, a Thai woman. One of the bar girls in my study, Hoi, had become attracted to other men while she was living with the foreigner who supported her. The professor, who sympathized with poor women who had no choice but to become prostitutes, thought my depiction of Hoi made all the bar girls look evil. She said I should have used another woman as an example. The professor could understand Hoi's selling her body, but she wouldn't give Hoi the right to have sex with a man just because she liked him. Even though Hoi was a paid companion, she was supposed to be faithful to the man who was paying. A Thai woman was supposed to repress her desires, whether she was a wife or a prostitute.

Online, I've seen how easy it is for men to upload GIFs of their penises. They are proud of them. If I put naked photos of myself on my homepage, I'd expect negative reactions. I envy the freedom men have to be sexual and to express their arousal.

When I'd investigated the blow-job bars on Patpong, I hated the shame that society encoded in me, which stopped me from spreading my legs in public and paying a cute Thai guy to bring me to orgasm. I wasn't born with that shame. It was forced into my programming against my will. When I lived in Goa, the Goa freaks were naked on the beach all day. The women went topless to the flea markets while sporting stylish skirts and floppy hats, and it never bothered me to be naked outdoors either.

But once I came back to the United States, after six years of nakedness, the shame of nudity returned in weeks. The way other women looked away in the health-club locker room and the horror on someone's face when I mentioned I didn't wear underwear brought back the old conditioning as if it had never gone.

Seeing the CUseeme men so willing to broadcast their erections made me aware of the "shame chip" in my brain's hardware. I resented it. It came from society telling women they didn't have the right to be sexual, that they weren't supposed to enjoy sex or want it.

One time, Chiba opened a new MOO, this one in Sydney, Australia. I'd worn out my creativity for Patpong and prostitutes. I needed a new theme. I reached into my past to my teenage years. When I was seventeen, I wrote a column about the music scene in New York, which put me in contact with rock bands coming from England. Eventually I fell in love with a rock star and he with me. I made two trips to England to visit him during Christmas and summer breaks from school, and he bought me an engagement ring. Alas, our union was not destined to last. In those days I hung out at a club called The Scene, and there happened to be another woman named Cleo there. One month, *Time* magazine wrote an article about "groupies." They interviewed the other Cleo, who called herself a "super-groupie," and bragged about the famous musicians she'd slept with.

Unfortunately, the picture they published with the story featured me. Back in England, a catty secretary from my fiancé's record company had him sign a check on top of the magazine article. He noticed my picture and read the article. Feeling betrayed, he broke off the engagement. Hurt, angry, and needing revenge, I decided to become the most famous groupie ever. In reality I'd never considered myself a groupie. Most of my boyfriends had been musicians because that was the world I lived in.

I recorded a documentary album called the *Groupies Kiss and Tell*, produced by Alan Lorber; the following is a mention of the album in *Sir*, a '70s magazine that fell somewhere between *Playboy* and *Screw*.

A stereo LP has just been released that's guaranteed to cause no sacroiliac to sprain nor disc to slip while the listener jumps to the rhythm. In fact, this unusual record offers no music at all. It's all talk—girl talk.

Super Status. Such crass approaches are unnecessary for the grandes dames of groupie society, the Super Groupies. Beautiful, usually intelligent, often well-heeled, they are welcome—in fact, sought-after—company. "They live the life that every other so-called groupie aspires to—spending this week with one top group, next week with another, maybe traveling to London or Jamaica," says Steve Paul, owner of The Scene, a Manhattan rock club. Paul estimates that "no more than ten" groupies actually qualify for super status.

Like the women who gravitated to the 19th century British Romantic poets, they are artistic as well as physical help-meets. Songs are written for them and about them; they act as critics and even co-composers. "It's all one big ego trip," gushes Super Groupie Cleo, a strawberry blonde 18-year-old New Yorker who is a look-alike for Jane Fonda. (*Time*, 2/28/69:48)

Titled "The Groupies," the album was recorded during a marathon 10-hour intimate conversation among four girls. They gabbed at length—and in explicit detail—about rock musicians, drugs and, above all, their sex lives.

Girls have always gone wild over musicians but today's *groupies* differ considerably from their predecessors. They are willing to deal directly with that nervousness they often feel when listening to rock groups. Frequently, this means jumping into bed with whatever artist happens to be her favorite at the moment—or whichever one happens to be closest to hand.

A groupie's approach is apt to be brazen. Wasting few words, she may ask the musician to sleep with her. Sometimes even this preliminary is dispensed with. More than one rock star has returned to his hotel room to discover a gate-crashing groupie awaiting him in bed.

Chances are she won't stay there long. Thanks in part to the Pill—which few groupies from fifteen to forty-five would try to do without—girls often change bed partners quicker than partners are swung on a square-dance floor. (Hudson, 1970: 11)

I made guest appearances on TV talk shows, like David Susskind's and Alan Burke's, to promote the album. I don't know if revenge is exactly what I ended up with, but becoming a celebrated groupie was fun. I was even given a free pass to the Woodstock festival that said: *Affiliation— groupie*.

On *The David Susskind Show*, taped October 5th, 1969, where I was on a panel of five "groupies," Susskind kept asking us questions with a moral bent or an insinuation that something was wrong with what we were doing. He hinted that our promiscuity would afflict us forever and that we lacked pride in our bodies. He wondered about our being "used up," and even suggested that our behavior was really just an act of parental defiance. Sex, apparently, was regarded as a zero-sum game—the female lost something, the male won.

The engagement breakup was my first encounter with cultural disparities between male and female sexuality. The musicians were applauded for their easy access to women wherever they entertained. Having groupies offering sexual favors spawned envy in every male. On the other hand, society frowned on women who chalked up famous rock-star lovers. I was baffled when Alan Burke blamed and scolded American motherhood for allowing groupies to happen. Many a male movie character gains the viewers' admiration for his achievement in scoring with a particular woman, going after her by hook or by crook or by a daring rescue, and winning her affection in the end. The sailor with a sweetheart in every port, the pilot with one in every city, and the trucker with a string of gas-stop gals, are all symbols of the successful manly male. So why couldn't groupies be revered for their conquests?

The message that men were allowed to be sexual but women were not was incorporated unnoticed and unchallenged into my worldview. Despite this, as a child I identified more with my father's boisterousness and drive than my mother's helplessness and frivolity. It never dawned on me that I was "supposed" to act like a female, and that the blue Smurfette was my role model. When I reached the point where I had to establish who I was as Cleo, I finally rejected what my mother tried to impose and searched for traits that better suited me. I was shocked to realize what part of me had always known, that a particular behavior could be seen as male or female.

In the circles I traveled in, the men slept with as many women as they wanted, and obliviously, I did the same thing. Since the whole hippie culture of the time was viewed by the older generation as deviant, I steadfastly ignored their criticism.

Now when I find something that pushes my shame button, I get angry at the culture that instilled it in me without giving me a pop-up window option that asked if I wanted to "install."

Cyberspace helps me chip away at that installed sexual-shame program, though even now I am unable to delete it completely.

To society, the worst use of sex, of course, is as a means to an end that's not socially sanctioned, i.e., as prostitution, which is perhaps why I fought so hard to have the Patpong prostitutes recognized for their strength and courage and for the economic contributions they made to their home villages.

Though I'd first encountered the sexual-rights disparity during the groupie adventures of my adolescent years, it didn't really sink in until decades later. I now see that the people back then wouldn't accept the fact that a female could think "I want sex with that guy" and then actually do it. People acted as if a woman would only have sex in exchange for something, whether it was marriage or money. The following is from the transcript of a WRVR radio roundtable I participated in on October, 2, 1969, dis-

> Part of the job of being a prostitute is to be used as a sign to other women of where the bottom is—to be labeled a whore and an unfit mother . . . a loose woman. So that part of the work of being a prostitute is to be made an example of what it costs us to refuse the poverty . . . to be the whip against other women to make sure that they strive always to be "respectable" though poor. And this means that part of the work of being a prostitute must also be living with not only the contempt but the envy of other women for having the little bit of money, the little bit of independence, that they don't have. (Brown, 1977:1)

cussing groupies who chose rock stars they wanted to have sex with:

> GUESTS: Cleo a "groupie"; Jean Baer author of *Single Girl Goes to Town*; Kate Millet, author of the essay in *American Review #7* "Sexual Politics, Miller, Mailer and Genet"; Dr. Eugene Borowitz; author of *Choosing a Sex Ethic*, professor of education, New York School of Hebrew Union College; host, Cyril Peterson; topic, The Sex Image: Truth or Myth.

> Borowitz: But, there was also a great desire on their part not to be thought of as either cheap or as whores. And that is why they were not interested in having goods particularly. It is somehow felt that if one trades one's sexuality for companionship, and status, and perhaps occasional gifts of money, that's allowed. That gives one a certain degree of personal dignity. Whereas if one was simply a prostitute, that would not. I must confess, I had the same reaction you did. It seems to me, the prostitution is here, only the kind of economics of prostitution has changed.

Baer: Well, in a way, it's a certain voluntary—

Borowitz: One doesn't go into voluntary slavery, at least my point of view not thinking that music is the whole world, or terribly significant as a matter of fact.

Millet: Well, music's great. But it has nothing to do with the status of the groupie, and particularly her acceptance of her own situation.

Cleo: I don't see how it can be associated with prostitution when they want to do it.

Borowitz: A prostitute's willing to do it, too, for a certain kind of exchange. And the difference between a prostitute, it would seem to me, and this kind of thing, is only that very often a prostitute doesn't have any particular interest in the act itself, only in the exchange. . . .

On the other hand, one thing that can be said here for the girls is that they apparently enjoy the sex itself. But what they're also doing is exchanging the sexual partnership that they give for certain kinds of rewards. And if they don't get the rewards, they won't do it. Girls would not go out with men with short hair. If the guy is not an important guy in the music business, he's not giving anything in exchange. So, while it's ethical to the extent that at least they're enjoying the sex, and they're doing it voluntarily, they're measuring fairly closely the kind of return they're getting. Now we see that in every level, not just with groupies. We see it in marriages, we see it in people who live with one another, we see it with people who go out with one another. It's a kind of a trading off. And it's this trading of sex as a commodity, as a thing to be used, which I think is so important, which in Ms. Millet's article I found so marvelously exposed. Namely, in what should be a very deep—now I'm speaking in my own ethical terms— what should be a very deep and human personal interrelationship, what we have is an exchange of power of one kind or another: "I have the power to give you a good time; you have the power to give me status; now let us bargain this away in ways which seem to be reasonably acceptable to us as contrasted to love."

The idea that a woman had sex with someone simply because she wanted to was just not an accepted concept. Today's society has not changed that much. A look at contemporary talk-shows finds people still shaming young women for their sexual behavior and carrying forward the warning that males only want them for sex and will lose respect for them once they get it.

After being unable to get Mars on video, and after an Echo crash that kept me from the Palace and reintroduced me to the Sex Room on Lambda MOO, I met someone with whom I had several days of role-playing sex. Though I'd progressed enough to engage in various types of online sex, he was more comfortable than I was in suggesting a role for us to play. The shame chip made me hesitate to reveal the fantasy scenes that turned me on. This bothered me.

One day when I found him in the Den of Love. I poked him and said, *I have an idea.*

Oh? Do tell me :)

Do you CUseeme?

He didn't have a camera, but he must have heard about CUseeme because his imagination of what we could do with video took off and soon he said, *I'm downloading CUseeme now. I won't be able to get a camera till next week, though. In the meantime I can watch YOU.*

The shame monster loomed before me. I felt it and hated it. NO! You are not me, you were forced on me without my consent and I'm going to vanquish you, shame monster.

The cyber lover lived in England, and by the time I returned from my office, it would be the middle of the night for him on a workday. But he was so enthralled that he was eager to C-me anyway. I was determined to seize the opportunity to overcome my gender conditioning. I wanted to break the barrier that made me embarrassed of my genitals. What a stupid emotion embarrassment was.

After adjusting camera angle and lighting, I put on a wig to keep my face hidden—vanquishing shame didn't mean I was going to open myself up to blackmail or ridicule if the other person wanted to put a nude picture of me on the Web.

That night I succeeded in further freeing my sexuality from the shackles of society. I let myself be the sexual being I am and let myself enjoy the pleasure my body was capable of without embarrassment or shame.

What freedom! What power! I slew a dragon!

5. Addiction/Obsession/Love

▶ Unlike Jules (Chapter 3), I'm prone to both obsession and jealousy in RL and VR. And I certainly have an addictive personality, though I try to channel my addictions into worthwhile things. To me, cyberspace is definitely worthwhile. Almost every day in Harry's Bar, we joke about our addiction to the Palace. As we encourage guests to become members, we also warn them that the Palace is like a Roach Motel—you come in but you never go out.

To many MOOers, the MOO is not "virtual" anything—it's real and the characters are real, whether they fly through the air, lay claim to royalty, or present themselves as a different gender. My first few months on the MOO were great fun, like finding a new toy. Later, though, I became afraid. My fear wasn't in finding myself addicted but was in finding myself, period. With the help of my academic background, I began to realize that my emotional responses, my historic traumas, my insecurities, and other assorted "monsters" were being revealed to me through the computer medium. I've parachuted out of airplanes, scuba dived to a hundred feet beneath the sea, and traveled through Iran as a lone female, but nothing scared

Nevertheless, some people are definitely hurting themselves by their addiction to computers and cyberspace. When people lose their jobs, or flunk out of school, or are divorced by their spouses because they cannot resist devoting all of their time to virtual lands, they are pathologically addicted. These extreme cases are clear-cut. But as in all addictions, the problem is where to draw the line between "normal" enthusiasm and "abnormal" preoccupation.

"Addictions"—defined very loosely—can be healthy, unhealthy, or a mixture of both. If you are fascinated by a hobby, feel devoted to it, would like to spend as much time as possible pursuing it—this could be an outlet for learning, creativity, and self-expression.

Even in some unhealthy addictions you can find these positive features embedded within (and thus maintaining) the problem. But in truly pathological addictions, the scale has tipped. The bad outweighs the good, resulting in serious disturbances in one's ability to function in the "real" world. . . .

As yet, there is no official psychological or psychiatric diagnosis of an "Internet" or "Computer" addiction. The most recent (4th) edition of *Diagnostic and Statistical Manual of Mental Disorders* (a.k.a., *DSM-IV*)—which sets the standards for classifying types of mental illness—does not include any such category. It remains to be seen whether this type of addiction will someday be included in the manual. (Suler, August 1996) me so much as a look at my emotional ghosts, and the fear that is part of them. The fear you feel as a bus near-misses you is very different from the fear you find within yourself.

The need for love, the obsessive attachment to some name on the screen, jealousy, illogical rage—all these were far scarier than realizing I was a net junkie.

But in the same way that the first cigarette puff initiates a cough and distaste but is followed by pleasure and addiction, I soon adjusted and forgot about my misgivings in the excitement of MOOing. Unease returned occasionally when overpowering emotions welled up, but I told myself I needed the information for research and talked myself into staying involved. The MOO is irresistible. One teenage MOOer's family sent him to a psychiatrist because he'd dropped out of school to spend more time online.

The MOO is compelling and can take over people's lives. They spend every possible moment on the MOO, giving up food and sleep. I lost ten pounds during my first two MOO months because I couldn't eat and type at the same time.

I've watched dust balls grow in my apartment and laundry accumulate until I had more clothes in the hamper than in the closet. The ever-present busy signal discouraged friends from trying to phone me. A total Internet junkie, I didn't get off the computer until my wrists ached. Typing for long hours caused repetitive-stress injury. One MOOer described her wrist pain as feeling like a crucifixion. My longest MOO session was eighteen hours straight, but my friend The_Necromancer has done twenty hours without a break, and thirteen hours on a regular basis is

> ... one of the reasons why [the] MOO is so addictive to some people. It offers a relief from the stresses of their normal life. It can offer you someone to talk to and complain to who is outside of your problems, people who have no expectations from you, and the opportunity to do almost anything that you can imagine and might not be able to do in real life. It offers freedom. (Rosenberg, 1992)

fairly typical for serious MOOers. Louis, a regular of Lambda's Sex Room, told me he spends at least three hours a day there, mostly hanging out in the main gathering spot. If he finds a partner and starts a sexual scenario in a private room, it could last another three hours.

Only when every letter I typed brought agony to my wrists, did I force myself to log off. But not for long. Eventually, I paid a handyman to nail a keyboard shelf to the underside of my desk drawer for a better typing position. It was hideous and inconvenient, since I could no longer open the drawer, but cutting down on online time was not an option.

Addiction to net sex is different from addiction to net browsing in that it has the additional component of being physically arousing, compelling the user to endless searching for a sexual encounter, usually more than one, and then another one and another one. Net addiction, therefore, can't be lumped into one category. Some MOOers like to program, some like to chat, some to cyberslut, and some, like me, are hooked by all three.

For a study on computer addiction, a survey was posted on CompuServe and the Internet and the "responses indicated that life on line can be habit forming."

Twenty-two reported experiencing "a cocaine rush" from their mastery of online technology. Twelve others said the electronic conversations lulled them.

"My days are hectic and loud, but the hours I spend online are quiet and private. For me, being online is like smoking pot." — Marcy

The substance analogies may not be coincidental. Nearly half the respondents said they were addicts. "I'm hooked. If you hear of a 12-step program for online abusers let me know." — Miriam

Addictive personalities, obsessive people, tend to gravitate toward computers in the first place, said Paul Gillin, the editor of *Computer World*. (O'Neill, 1995)

Net addicts sometimes feel guilty about the time they spend online. Before I found cyberspace, though, I'd come home from work and veg out in front of the TV. Now I'm at the computer until an hour before bedtime, an hour needed to quiet my brain for sleep. Unless it takes time away from necessary activities, I don't view living in cyberspace as a bad thing, though some may disagree.

Sometimes I feel lust free-floating within me, just waiting for someone to attach itself to. It feels kind of dangerous. I wish I fell only for rich, successful, kind, sensitive men, but alas, I'm more likely to go for the long-haired hobo sleeping in the park. When I feel myself in this vulnerable state, like a passion arrow looking for a target, I think, "Uh-oh, I better watch whose company I keep." That damn arrow has dragged me into enough trouble in the past.

But I've also succeeded in using this awareness to influence the arrow somewhat. I'd once been crazy-obsessed with the twenty-eight-year-old MOO man named Mars. After our first bout of net sex, I was as consumed by him as I imagine Amy Fisher was by Joey Buttafuoco. I checked to see when Mars had last logged on, how long he'd been on, and if he'd added a female name to his "pals" list. On the MOO you have a "pals" file and add to it with the command @pal. Whenever you log on, you'll be told which of your pals are online and how long they've been idling. Scanning someone's pal list can be informative. Other spy commands tell you his location and the names of people he's with. If I found Mars in his bedroom with a female character, I went nuts with jealousy. If I found him alone but idle for even a few seconds, I imagined him paging a female, which also made me nuts with jealousy. Being idle for a short time meant the person was actively MOOing, as opposed to those who've been idle two to eight hours. The spy locator would tell me if Mars was in the "editor," fixing or writing something. If not editing, he had to be communicating with someone.

Ugh. I was aghast at my compulsive search for his whereabouts. I hate obsessing. I could understand my possessiveness when it was for Jagwire, with whom I had a relationship, but when I found it directed at Mars, I couldn't justify it at all. Not all people have this trait of possessiveness. I was surprised when Louis told me that if he fancied a lady but found her with someone else, *I'll just wait and give her space*—a behavior incomprehensible to me.

I'd learned from previous episodes that the fastest way to get rid of an online obsession was to absolutely, positively, under no circumstances, allow myself to look for the person. This was the only way to make the compulsion subside, even if it meant not doing a general "look" to see who was online. This depravation is pretty drastic since the first thing most people do when they enter a virtual space is see who else is there. When I was recovering from the Echo romance with Jeremy Berg, after finally admitting he wasn't Narayan, I still had an urge to watch his movements. So I forbade myself to look for Jeremy. It worked. A great source of anxiety vanished.

When I wanted to get over my MOO obsession with Mars, I took this first step. I admonished myself: "Cleo, do not @look to see who's on Lagda." I'd also gotten into the habit of !fingering Mars's ISP (Internet Service Provider) to see when he'd last connected. He could have been elsewhere on the net besides the MOO. The "!finger" command allows you to peek into another online service. You could !finger the person or !finger the whole provider, which would present you with a list of everyone connected at that moment. I forced myself to stop investigating the details of Mars's life. Unfortunately, the craving to @look and !finger was powerful. So I attempted a mind trick. Since I'd been communicating flirtatiously with Peter in Thailand, I decided to see if I could transfer my feeling from Mars to him. Instead of checking for Mars, I started checking for Peter on @mozart.inet.co.th in Thailand. I !fingered his ISP whenever I felt compelled to !finger Mars. Eventually @mozart disallowed remote !fingers, and I giggled, imagining it was a reaction to all the pokes it had received from me.

Amazingly, my trick worked. Within days I had transferred my obsession from one person to another. What a relief. On the other hand, it made me feel like a mindless robot to be able to switch so easily a pathway in my brain, like flipping a track switch so a train goes north instead of south. It's disconcerting to find myself so programmable and at times I question how fine the distinctions are between humans and computers.

Janet, who's continued her relationship with her boyfriend in England via the computer for four years, is also a jealous and obsessive type. When she suspected another woman was flirting with her man in a news group, she lashed out at the woman viciously. She flamed her and later felt shame when she learned that the fear underlying the jealousy (of the loss of her love to someone else) was based on an impossibility.

In RL and VR, Janet and I are jealous types; in RL and VR, Jules and Louis are not. This is not a gender trait, though; I've heard from plenty of men who were obsessed over a women, and TV reports of male stalkers also attest to it.

Fred is a self-proclaimed cyber-sex addict. After two years he recently canceled all his Internet accounts and claims to be "in recovery." His journey began with phone sex. Role-playing was his favorite sexual activity. "During phone sex," he told me, "most of the call consisted of an elaborate story, which led to the sex scene, which was the denouement. Very rarely did I just get down to it when she answered the phone."

But then Fred got married and there were fewer opportunities for him to continue his phone play.

"And then I discovered cyber sex. It was silent. It afforded even more possibilities for role-playing. I found myself hurrying through the rest of my life so I could get back to it.

"Did I ever MOO as a guest? Yes. My character was pretty well established, so being a guest allowed me to play other sorts of roles. I also enjoyed seducing women who had already been with my character."

I asked Fred if he had physical orgasms during cyber sex.

"Not very often, actually. Though I would be excited, manipulating myself, and typing with one hand, sometimes hours on end. I would usually wait until I logged off to climax. There were a few exceptions. And often those exceptions had to do with how much the role-playing scene was exciting me, rather than the sex part. This is in direct contrast to the phone, where I would usually climax at least once, often more, during every call. I enjoy the phone more than cyber sex. Sound is important to me. Additionally, I only have to keep one hand on the phone. The mechanics of the whole thing are easier."

But now he is on the wagon. Compulsive cyber sexing so overwhelmed his life, he had to take this drastic step of canceling all his accounts.

Greg is another MOO sex addict. He has about four sex partners a week as his character, but he goes on as a guest, too. He's met two of his MOO lovers in RL. They both came to spend a weekend with him. He had RL sex with both and called both "fat." The relationship didn't continue with either afterward. Greg has obsessed over an occasional MOO woman, and he's found it necesarry to seek therapy because of his cyber life. He's still at it, though he sometimes manages to stay away for a few weeks or months. It's common to find people forcing themselves off the net for a period of time as they find themselves without an RL and too much of a V one.

Aside from addiction to cyberspace, addiction to net sex is not rare. I know of many who are in this position, and have been there myself.

After Fractal_Muse and Stormwatch, university students on separate continents, met and fell in love on the Sprawl MOO, they arranged to meet in RL. Together in person for only a week, they decided their love was true and they continued the relationship on the MOO after Stormwatch returned to England. A few months later they posted a wedding invitation:

Date: Fri. Apr. 28 05:25:12 1995
From: Fractal_Muse
Subject: You are cordially invited . . .
    You are cordially invited to the MOOwedding
of Stormwatch and Fractal_Muse. This wedding
is a celebration of the love they share, and the
special place where they met, namely Chiba-

MOO—the Sprawl. They wish to have all their friends in attendance as they form a bond which, while not taking the place of the vows they will exchange in three years in real life, will still form a lasting bond between them, a bond as real as the ring Fractal wears on her left hand in real life.

The wedding will be held on Sunday, May 7, 1995, in the Clearing in the Woods at 8 pm EST. This is midnight GMT, and 5 pm MOOtime (PST). The ceremony will be performed by the ArchMagus Beradan, a treasured friend of the couple.

Fractal and Stormwatch look forward to your attendance.

The wedding was romantic. The MOOer named Beradan orchestrated the ceremony and Fractal_Muse and Stormwatch said "I do" at the right moments. We spectators uttered comments and reactions such as: *Patpong sobs; Nordic_Wolf wipes tears from his eyes; Gilly says, "This is so beautiful"; Rocker sniffs.* The occasional "arrival message" such as *Grood_Dragon flies in on a toaster* added MOO ambience.

Alas, the couple broke up within six months of matrimony. Stormwatch changed his name and Fractal_Muse refused to discuss what had happened. They never again met in person.

When you're in MOO love, you check repeatedly to see if the person is online, if he's with a female, and if he's wearing his MOO clothes. A "naked message" is a sure sign your beau is sowing virtual seeds elsewhere. Net love can happen without the couple ever seeing pictures of each other, without ever talking on the phone. Yet the obsession is there and so is the passion.

Mellisa, twenty-three years old at the time, told me about her net romance with someone on the opposite side of the planet:

"I was @created on ChibaMOO amidst the Newbie Boomers of Spring Break '95. I believe I was a bright and quick-learning young newbie. I learned to program when I was only three days old.

"My story is linked to the stories of the other MOOers on ChibaMOO, for what affected others had impacts on my MOO life as well. When I was a young MOOer, I used to hang out in #11, Sprawl City Limits. It was there I learned the basics of MOO—how to walk, how to talk, how to spoof, and netiquette in general. It was here that I also met my first MOO love. An ominously quiet avatar named Spherical hit me with my first can of 'Spam.' From that moment on, I knew I had to learn to program so I could get revenge.

"Spherical became my mentor in MOO programming, teaching me how to @dump things, to look at their interiors, their code, and how they worked.

"As a young MOOer, I was materialistic and quota-greedy. Back in those days a purple tiger named Baloo, an immigrant from Lambda MOO, was in charge of the petitions for quota raises, and I discussed with him at great length how I could get 1,000K as several other MOOers had.

"@auditing all the programmers I could find, I discovered StarDancer. As she was not the socialite type, I had to go to her to meet her. She resided in the 'Freeside Docking Bay' (named after the space station in William Gibbons's book *The Neuromancer*, a MOOer's bible). I had interesting discussions with her about everything from coding to poetry. Most interestingly, we discussed MOO in detail, as if it were a life of our own, and because of her, MOO did indeed become an integral part of my life. Although I never met her in real life, she became one of my good friends.

"Meanwhile, Spherical and I also became good friends, and I found myself obsessed with the idea of going to see him in his home country, New Zealand, which is on the other side of the globe from me. Our relationship was like a dream sequence in a soap opera and totally non-physical, purely intellectual. We would spend our time together discussing ideas, brainstorming, dreaming, and sometimes playing Scrabble or chess.

"Cohabiting with him on the MOO was something I hesitated to do. As MOO seemed to mimic real life very vividly for me, I hesitated to @move in with someone to whom I was not MOO married. It became a situation of my deciding if real-life morals applied in a place where the corporeal world had no bearing.

"I eventually did @sethome in his 'place,' and discovered that merely knowing that your avatar is snuggled safely with your MOO love every night gives you a lot of emotional support. It was also pleasant to 'wake up' (log on) and discover he had also 'waken up' earlier and left little love notes for me to read."

When I asked Mellisa about net sex, she first asked if

my definition included masturbation. When I told her no, she continued:

"How did I learn to have net sex? Well, my first book with sexual content was *The Shield of Three Lions* by Pamela Kaufman. That's how I learned that MOOers could be 'locked together . . . galloping harder and harder as the tangled trees whizzed above us and we panted in the effort to get where we were going . . . fermented honey bubbles exploded' and all that sort of stuff. In other words, net sex was the same as real sex for me. You could do it a number of ways, but it still felt generally the same.

"I used to think we were having net sex . . . Spherical and I. Then I heard that most MOOers believed that the definition of net sex included masturbating while online. However, I never needed to masturbate while Spherical and I exchanged sexual intent. On my side of the screen, the textual exchange was enough for me. I cannot say for sure whether or not he actually masturbated while we were having MOO intercourse. I honestly never really thought to ask!

"Oh wait! . . . I think once he asked me if I was masturbating while we exchanged sexual intent. I told him I didn't need to. It was fulfilling enough for me to be doing it purely in text. He seemed to find that strange. And looking back on it, it does seem rather strange, but true. I never had a traditional orgasm during MOO sex. However, text sex has a very intimate feeling for me, that is close to the real thing. Perhaps it's all in my imagination, but then again, perhaps RL sex has a lot to do with psyche as well. A lot of my pleasure came from knowing he was enjoying the exchange as much as I.

"And no, we didn't 'do' it every day. We exchanged kisses (if one can picture that over the net), or talked small cutesy talk. I'm sure many people think that it's akin to passing notes in elementary school to some guy you have a crush on. That's a good analogy . . . but it's not a perfect one. The real time interaction and the way actions are posed on the MOO made a big difference in how I interacted with him. We could actually 'go on dates' on the MOO. Go MOO hopping or play a board game or discuss a book together. I think the way we were forced to interact also made us careful of assuming what the other was trying to say, since typos are common and misunderstandings frequent. I ended up carrying that over into my next RL relationship, in which I tried not to jump to conclusions or respond too quickly to things that annoyed me without first hearing the other person's side of the story.

"While I was 'involved' with Spherical, I was still trying to learn MOO programming, and was continuously searching out MOO programmers who could help me with my ideas. I met one of these programmers, Jorgen, through StarDancer. Jorgen was always helpful, and articulate. Also, he seemed to love StarDancer as much as I did. I couldn't help thinking how cute it would be if they were MOO married, and suggested it several times to both of them. Unfortunately, just when I was thinking they had begun taking my suggestion in earnest, StarDancer was @toaded [killed as a character]. It caused many MOOers in ChibaMOO to be upset, including myself and Jorgen.

"While @toading is not equivalent to death in real life, it certainly does create an obstacle for further socializing with the @toaded. Being exiled from ChibaMOO, Star-

Dancer could only be reached elseMOO, i.e., laggy MOOs, which were not conducive to communication. Thus, I never saw much of her after her exile. ChibaMOO had become my home MOO, and I did not like to leave.

"Months after StarDancer's exile, my relationship with Spherical reached a plateau. My only explanation is that there are times when you crave the physical part of a relationship, and this was something we could not have. Although we made plans to see each other f2f, they always fell through due to real-life circumstances. It became a source of contention—who was not sacrificing enough so that the flesh-meet could go through? Furthermore, I was greedy for a picture of him, and he kept making excuses as to why he was not sending one. Also, we had never talked on the phone.

"Finally, six months into our MOO relationship, Spherical told me he had received a letter. His old flame, in real life, had written asking to meet him in northern New Zealand. We discussed whether or not he should go, and decided it would be best if he did. He promised he would keep his pants on and that he would tell me how it went.

"While he was away, Jorgen and I spent a lot of time together on the MOO. I had known him for six months, by this time. I knew that he was from my home state in the U.S., but had never planned to meet him in real life. He was merely a friend.

"However, something happened during the time that I spent with Jorgen, wondering if Spherical was 'keeping his pants on' and knowing that Jorgen was seven thousand miles closer to me than Spherical. My conscience fought with me. My MOO relationship with Spherical had become akin to a real-life marriage. I had made a commitment to him—a commitment made of recycled electrons, but a commitment nonetheless. Furthermore, I did not want to hurt StarDancer, who may have been keeping her eye on Jorgen and ChibaMOO's happenings from her home else MOO.

"I had previously seen Jorgen's picture on the Web, and knew he was not at all the unattractive geek that net junkies are made out to be. I also hid my picture in an archive on the net for him to see, and received a favorable response. Thrilled when he gave me his number, I gave in and actually talked to Jorgen on the phone.

"As we talked I began to see an unusual parallel in our story. Jorgen had liked me for some time, but had not said anything due to my relationship with Spherical. I had not admitted that I enjoyed his company because of his apparent interest in StarDancer.

"Thus, with former love interests out of the picture, we spent more time together on the MOO, and I was probably glowing more electrons than usual when Spherical returned.

"Strangely, Spherical told me he had not 'messed around' with his old flame. Their meeting had been purely platonic. I, however, admitted that I had spent quite some time with Jorgen during his absence. Spherical then gave me the guilt trip, saying, 'Well, I'm glad you didn't leave me for him while I was gone.'

"The days passed as Spherical and I continued our relationship where it had left off, but the sore spot remained. I could not join him in New Zealand. Thus, after many months of purely intellectual and emotional support, our relationship ended.

"After I broke up with Spherical, Jorgen and I contemplated whether or not it would work for us in RL. But in the end, we realized it wouldn't work out. So we never had net sex. We did 'kiss,' though. :)

"I think Jorgen and I didn't have casual net sex because we both felt the same way about MOO sex—that MOO relationships can be just as heartbreaking as real ones, and deserve just as much caution. Not all MOOers feel that way, but it's those MOOers that do take MOO life seriously that I tend to hang out with most.

"Do I still have net sex? Well, no. Perhaps because I have a significant other now. We don't do it often, either! If I hadn't met my current significant other, I think I may have continued to seek company. Not with just anyone, though, and not just on the net.

"On the MOO, I did not like to hang out in Hot Tubs or #11 waiting to be picked up, or actively 'looking.' I tended to 'talk' more to people with whom I had things in common. People who didn't seem to be 'looking' either. I didn't want to have net sex with anyone unless I thought there was a possibility of a lasting relationship. So the net was simply a place to meet 'interesting' people whom one might not normally meet."

6. Jealousy/Loss/Anger

▶ Loss and rejection is felt as vividly in virtual space as in real life. It's often an old wound that is reopened by a similar situation, letting the historic monsters out. Our past comes back painfully in this new way but hurts no less and, perhaps, may even be intensified in this medium that lacks physical reality checks on runaway imaginations.

Dworkin the wizard was devastated when World MOO, a SenseMedia MOO, collapsed due to an irreversible system's problem. Many of us citizens were dismayed at World's end, which can be seen in Dworkin's chronicling of his reaction. He was so upset that he published on the Web a six-page detailed account of his feelings, plus a harangue against Rocker, the owner of the MOO, and the SenseMedia corporation, which Dworkin called SenselessMedia. As testimony to the depth of his grief:

> If I were less reasonable than I am, I would take this time to suggest to Rocker which of his bodily orifices would be appropriate for the insertion of

WorldMOO, SenselessMedia, and any number of jagged pieces of metal. (Lodge, 1995)

It was just a MOO, a digitized place that many people wouldn't even acknowledge existed. But it existed inside Dworkin and it existed to us, its citizens.

When Jagwire and I were a couple, we had built a house for ourselves on World MOO. We'd shared in the house's creation and description. We felt heartache when we heard of the MOO's upcoming demise, announced two days beforehand. At 11:30 P.M., half an hour before World's end, we gathered with the others in the main MOO room. Jagwire and I shed tears. I can imagine Dworkin's sorrow to be much greater than ours. For Dworkin, that MOO was a progeny, like a seed from his loins.

Fortunately, the announcement of the death of the MOO gave me time to copy my work before it disappeared. When Rocker opened Snow MOO—named for the book *Snow Crash* (Stephenson, 1992), another MOOer's bible—I pasted Anjuna Beach back into the new space.

My friend StarDancer is a brilliant programmer. With her strong and quirky personality, she sometimes alienates the less knowledgeable MOOers. Though she's willing to help everyone, her technically advanced speech sometimes causes confusion. Then, if someone pesters her too much for clarification, she swats them like mosquitoes.

She battled Ice, the Sprawl MOO wizard, with whom she had no more patience than a newcomer.

A wizard should not be trifled with. They have their own monsters, and their monster of "entitlement" is nourished by, and grows fat on, their status.

In the end, StarDancer was deleted from the database of all SenseMedia MOOs and even some sister MOOs. Many of us loved StarDancer, though, and her execution incited a war that lasted weeks, dividing MOOers into hostile camps. Some people even resigned from Sprawl in protest. On top of the emptiness we felt without StarDancer, we were maddened that the fabulous things she'd programmed were deleted with her. With the removal of StarDancer's parent objects, we lost child objects. Loss is no less painful in VR than RL. The pang you feel when you come home to find your TV and VCR stolen is comparable to logging on to find something missing that you spent time programming and fine-tuning. My favorite object of StarDancer's was her "puppet" and I mourn it to this day. My bodyguard QT3.14 (pronounced cutie pie), a child of StarDancer's puppet, with several properties I'd tailored to protect me and to attack rude guests, was rendered useless when the parent puppet was deleted. Many of us wailed at the destruction of StarDancer's parent puppet, which resulted in the creation of a puppet cemetery.

It matters not whether the loss is "real" or "virtual," the emotional reaction is the same. Loss leaves an empty place inside you. The pain monster awakens and howls and reverberates throughout body and mind.

Who chooses what persona and why?

PrincessC was a young girl with cancer who logged in from her hospital bed. No one knew she was ill until, after becoming too sick to type, a few weeks before she died, she disappeared. Her cyber body still exists on Sprawl MOO in the "Room of Dead Things" and anyone can @look at the description she gave herself:

There was a little girl who had a little curl right in the middle of her forehead. When she was good, she was very, very good; but when she was bad, she was even better. ;)

She has been disconnected for 1 year, 5 months, 15 days, 21 hours, 55 minutes, and 40 seconds.

Her objects are still with her: *Objects owned by PrincessC—1K #3317 The Tower*

With an @examine of #3317, a description is given of the room she created:

The Tower—this is the home of PrincessC. It is a bit cold and drafty, but she is constantly search-ing for company to combat the loneliness and the cold winter wind.
Contents: flowers (#18059) Flower of Loss (#26816)

An *@examine* of #18059 and #26816 shows the de-scription of the flowers put there after she died:

#18059 flowers—flowers for the girl who is gone when she is only 19. When she was gone, everyone was mourning. Her friends will remember her —one of her friends

#26816 Flower of Loss—the name of this flower says it all.

The loss of a virtual friend is an RL loss as well.

An early member of the Palace, named Palace Geek, used a cartoon avatar of a geek with glasses. One day he used a photo of a cute blond guy, supposedly his real picture. Nice, but I had no romantic inclinations for him.

A few weeks later he switched to a wolf avatar and changed his name to Dakota. *I had trouble with the photo*, he told me. *I don't use it anymore because it got me in trouble with Sissy.* He said women were falling in love with him because of his picture. Hence, he was hiding.

Sissy? I answered, surprised. *But I thought Sissy was with Cobra Driver?*

I'd been friendly with Sissy and Cobra Driver. Though they lived on opposites sites of the United States, they'd met once and Cobra was due for another visit to New York—Sissy's home—to see her again. I planned to meet them both when he came. So I was confused that Palace Geek, now named Dakota, had trouble with Sissy being in love with him. But I didn't inquire further because I wasn't really motivated to do so.

Meanwhile, Dakota became attracted to me and followed me around the Palace. He changed back to the cute photo instead of the wolf. He whispered romantic poems to me. He told me he loved me. He pressed for a date when he could come to New York to meet me.

I avoided answering because I didn't want to meet him for a romantic weekend. Nevertheless, it was fun to play and flirt. Whenever I saw him, I rushed to his side, yelling, *DAK! DAK!* and used my kiss script, which changed my avatar to a photo of me with pursed lips and eyes closed, while activating the Palace's kissing sound. I wasn't interested in entering a lockable room with him for a private chat, though. I'd just become a wizard and preferred attending to wizard duties.

One day, I sat in my usual chair in the Red Room when Dakota entered. I flew to him with *DAK! DAK!* What a surprise—before the kiss was over, Dakota moved next to a woman named Robin, whose avatar was a picture of a pretty brunette.

Hey! I said in joking admonishment as I noticed I was kissing empty space, and before I had a chance to look around, *Where'd ya go?*

Suddenly Robin and Dakota were cheek to cheek and Dakota added a sign beneath his photo stating TAKEN. Robin popped the same sign under hers.

We're getting married next week, Robin announced to the room, *and you're all invited.* Dakota added, *The wedding will be at the end of March.*

Huh? They were getting married? But just the week before, Dakota whispered love poems to me! He'd given me a dog prop named Rex with a script that made him bark whenever someone said the word "Rex." Dakota called us a family—me, Dakota, and Rex.

His engagement affected me like a slap in the face—maybe because I felt like an idiot being left there kissing a blank space, maybe because I thought people would think I'd been dumped for Robin since Dakota and I had been often seen side by side.

Suddenly I was furious. I activated my BAD BAD BAD script, which had an angry face and a pointing finger, and used the Palace sound for "no"—a buzz similar to the wrong-answer sound on a TV game show.

Robin took a screen-shot "picture" of the two of them cheek to cheek and hung it on the wall. I was enraged.

But why? Was this a historic emotion? Did Dakota's actions recall old feelings from another situation? If so, I couldn't quite figure it out. I'm no stranger to jealousy. Was that what I was feeling, though? Jealousy? I felt like Dakota had discounted my feelings and thrown the relationship with Robin in my face. I didn't know if they were truly in a relationship, if they were having an RL wedding, a Palace wedding, or if they were just playing around. But so what even if it were true? If Dakota lacked sensitivity, so what?

"So what?" seemed the appropriate response, but a sore spot had been hit. I experienced an emotional upset that lasted days, darkening my every moment. What had I answered when Dakota suggested we meet in person? I couldn't remember. Probably something like, *Sure, one day if we're ever in the same state*. I didn't know where he lived because I hadn't been interested enough to remember. So why, if I'd never considered him a love object, did I feel betrayed?

I searched for an explanation. Someone said it was normal to be upset when you heard that a guy you weren't interested in was getting married, but I'd never reacted like that before. Maybe I was hurt by the way I'd found out about the affair. Dakota hadn't told me he'd been courting someone else—he just left me stranded, kissing air. He hadn't taken my feelings into consideration, a situation that did have historic connotations. My mother never took my feelings into consideration. Perhaps Dakota had ignited that old pain.

I was bursting with fury, and being a wizard, I had powers to use, maybe nothing that could control Dakota and Robin, but maybe I had influence to alter the situation. I felt uneasy at the image of myself as a vengeful person. Normally, I'd swallow hurt feelings and act as if nothing bothered me, but having power carries an irresistible urge to use it for personal ends.

The next night Dakota entered the Red Room. Robin wasn't there. I said, *Poo*. A friend asked, *What are you saying poo about?*

"*Poo, Dakota is here*," I answered.

Dakota left the room. Haha, I felt like a bitch, but I enjoyed expressing that bitchiness, showing I disapproved of him. As an authority figure, perhaps I could make him a persona non grata.

I tried to reason with myself to snap me out of the nastiness: "Cleo, you have a sensitive spot about people discounting your feelings, triggered by memories of your mother." Did that insight help? Not a bit.

In the following days of continuing anguish, I decided to ask Sissy about her and Dakota. Maybe I could prove he really was an insensitive brute, with no conscience, a danger to womankind.

I whispered to Sissy, *Dakota told me you were in love with him and that's why he changed his name.*

That's ridiculous! she answered. *I'm in love with Cobra Driver.*

Aha! Now I knew for sure he was a liar. Though I thought it wiser to resist the urge to attack, I decided to explore the freedom to act out hostile intentions that cyberspace offered. Should I tie Dakota to a virtual stake and roast him now that I could prove he'd lied?

The next encounter with Dakota was dramatic. I'd been hosting Harry's Bar when the subject of the wedding came up. I commented on its suddenness. River whispered to me that Robin had been wooing him, too.

Just then, Dakota entered. I couldn't control myself and called him a snake in a private message, *Sissy told me you lied about her, you piece of shit.* Then, horror of horrors, after whispering to me that he was sorry if he'd hurt me (which enraged me even more because now I really felt like the scorned woman), he shouted to the room: *ATTENTION. MAY I HAVE EVERYONE'S ATTENTION FOR A MINUTE!*

The room quieted as fifteen people said, *Sure.* I knew Dakota was going to say something about me and I wanted to run from the room. But I couldn't. I did the next wimpiest thing—I said, *Phone. Be right back*, a phrase heard often on the Palace. People frequently say *be right back* when an RL situation—phone call, need for the bathroom, doorbell—calls their attention away from the computer. I couldn't remember if I'd told Dakota I had only one phone line, thereby making a phone call impossible.

Just as I'd feared, he began: *I want to tell you all about someone I consider a very special person.*

I wanted to crawl under the bar's Oriental rug. He was giving a consolation speech, like the I-consider-you-a-good-friend you tell someone whose affection you don't share.

Dakota continued, *I want everyone to know what a special person I consider Cleo to be.*

When the speech ended, I said, *Back,* the usual thing people say when they return to their keyboard after being elsewhere.

I felt relieved when Dakota noted, *Here I've been saying all these nice things about her and she wasn't even here.*

Aloud I said, *Aw, that's so sweet of you. Thanks.* In private I said to him: "Fuck you." Then I added the whisper, *From what I've heard about Robin, you two deserve each other.*

What did you hear? he asked.

She's been after a lot of guys and recently.

Who? he demanded to know. I loved the emotion I imagined in his tone.

Fortunately, the man was still in the room. *Ask River,* I whispered back. *He's right here.*

Dakota was quiet awhile, and I guessed he was speaking privately to River. I felt like a vicious bitch.

Suddenly, in capital letters, Dakota announced to the room: *THE WEDDING IS OFF.*

To me, he said, *Thanks Cleo.* Was that sarcastic? I

couldn't tell. Nevertheless, I was pleased to death the wedding was off. Dakota left the room and disconnected.

Pure raw emotions, within ourselves, those are our demons. Jealousy, insecurity, longings, and lust have frequently spooked me by jumping out of hidden spots in my brain. Though I'd had no romantic interest in Dakota, his "unfaithfulness" hit a nerve. I wasn't proud of my inability to restrain the nasty words aimed at preventing the wedding from happening, but I was pleased at their success.

After the wedding had been canceled, a few of the wizard women got together with Robin to discuss how Dakota had been lying and to offer friendship and support. I told Robin my impression of Dakota as a snake. I tried to be honest about my feelings but caught myself placing more blame on Dakota's actions than on my reactions. As I ranted about Dakota's courting various lovers simultaneously, a twinge of guilt reminded me that I did that myself. Afterward, Robin and I became Palace friends. Dakota was never seen again, though I suspected he was there but with a new name and appearance.

A few months later, after an RL romantic interlude and a few VR ones, I laughed at the ridiculous feelings during the Dakota–Robin crisis. By that time the monster had dissolved. When I received email from Dakota saying he apologized for what he'd done, that he was ashamed of his behavior, and that he'd erased the Palace from his hard drive, I answered with an *Aw, come back to us.*

The next day, I saw Robin online and gave her a nice greeting. She whispered back, *Thank you for helping me through the marriage ordeal.* Then she said, *I'm not com-*

ing online anymore. I'm dying. I have multiple sclerosis. I'm going to the hospital tomorrow.

Robin was dying of MS? Oh shit! What a brute I felt like for being catty and ruining her wedding. But was this true? PrincessC had been dying in RL while leading a full virtual life, but I'd been around long enough not to believe everything I heard online.

On the other hand, if Robin truly was sick with MS while I tangoed with my jealousy monster and acted like a witch, then I felt especially cruel for destroying what could have been a pleasant experience for her.

I just got email from Dakota yesterday, I told Robin. *It was strange. I hadn't heard from him for months and all of a sudden he sounded abashed and apologetic.*

Oh, she answered. *That's probably because I'd just sent him an angry letter.*

I didn't press for details about what she'd written him, but it must have made him feel bad enough that he e-mailed me an apology.

In any case, Robin did continue to show up at the Palace, but now she was talking about suicide because she was so sick. Again, I didn't immediately believe that this was true.

Identity is important, so I was not surprised the first time a Palace member complained that someone stole her avatar. The puppy face Mandy had created represented her personhood, her existence as a human being on planet Earth. People knew her as that puppy. When a man wore the avatar, even though he used his own name, Mandy felt victimized. She was so upset she almost quit the Palace forever. She'd lost her identity.

In truth, anyone can do a screen capture and edit out an avatar. Nobody's is guaranteed. After that first crisis, it happened again and the issue was brought up on the wizards' discussion list. It was our job as wizards to look at an issue, appraise it, and decide if the medium could sustain the social value it manifested. People's sense of self anchors them to the world. Their name, home, family, job, friends, and hobbies center them in an identity, a base from which to deal with others and from which stems social responsibility. In cyberspace, your name, appearance, and personality cement you to your online community. Unlike the MOO, name and creations are not permanently stored on the Palace database.

As innocent as taking someone's face may seem, it can cause emotional distress. People feel violated, as if their physical body had been tampered with. Meddling with people's identity provokes a monster in them. Our cyber images are plugged into our self-images.

When I was fifteen, I changed my name to Cleo because I felt invisible to my mother, and there was such a gulf between who I was and who my mother imagined I was that I needed to express, "This is me. I'm not that other person." I never tell anyone my original name. To me, that person never existed. I'm Cleo.

My name and what it represented was so significant that I didn't respond when called anything else, no matter what the cost. If a friend used the wrong name, I ended the relationship. Some idiosyncrasies from early life are survival tactics. Flooded with expectations from my mother and unseen for who I was, I fended off the confusion of conflicting personalities by clinging to one—me, Cleo—disassociating from the others. From the identity of self comes inner strength.

When impersonations became a topic on the wizards' list, I understood the importance of protecting someone's online persona from thieves. From the grieving cries for help, the other wizards realized that face and name stealing was a problem. In the end, we concluded that we'd make it clear that stealing avatars, or using someone's name when he or she wasn't connected, could happen, but that we'd try to make the thief aware that someone's feelings were hurt in the process. A virtual culture tries to mirror the values of its citizens, but this was a tough one to enforce by reprimand alone. The problem called for a technical solution, an identity protector written into the software.

On the MOO we program "verbs," for example, hiss, thwap, and strip. Weapons are the most prolific *verbs*—those and the lovey-dovey ones (the basics of war and love). MOOers test their battle verbs on each other. I've written attack verbs to protect myself but also to annoy others when I'm crotchety. My wickedest creation is an asp with the verb "bite," inspired by a fit of jealousy. I send the asp into a room where the target is with a female, hoping to disrupt the sex act I imagine is taking place. Though a room is locked, I can @move the asp into it and set it in motion with the command "bite playername with asp."

I sent it to Jagwire once when I spied him in a room with a female named Zeden. Though our MOO romance had long been over and my desire for him gone, I still harbored resentment from the times during our affair when he'd sent me mispages. Innocent though they were, private messages meant for another woman mistakenly sent to me had infuriated me, and the ill will they roused still lingered. The jealousy monster that had been called up had not totally dissipated, though my desire for Jagwire had.

On that day, Jagwire and Zeden saw these messages with a ten-second pause between each sentence:

Cleopatra's asp teleports in. Cleopatra's asp lands on Jagwire's head. The asp slithers down Jagwire's chest and creeps between his legs. Cleopatra's asp bites off the tip of Jagwire's dick.

Oh, what fun I've had with that asp. I can castrate a man with my cyber fangs.

Jules does not get jealous or obsessed in RL or VR. Janet, who continued her R and V relationship with her boyfriend in England for years, gets both jealous and obsessed. When Janet found a woman whose postings in a news group appeared to be flirtatious toward her boyfriend, she attacked the woman viciously and openly for all to read.

Louis also gets jealous. Once, he was flirting with a woman in the Hot Tub on Lambda MOO. The woman was responding favorably. They seemed to be drawing to-

> On its more negative side, the disinhibiting effect of computer-mediated communication encourages the expression of dissent, rebellion, hostility, and anti-social chaos. It involves a stripping away of the social coordinates that let the user know where he or she is in the cultural network, indeed it encourages this by allowing the continual invention of new moves to old language games. (Reid, 1991)

gether. Louis became attached to her. Suddenly the woman's RL boyfriend came online in his MOO character and the woman left the Hot Tub to join him. Louis was so consumed with jealousy and anger that he paged the woman, *Now I know why men kill women*, and paged the man, *You should leash that bitch*. Louis told me, *I really scared her with what I said. I felt awful afterward—that I'd been so cruel.*

Irrational anger and the phenomenon of "flames" and "flame wars" are unique to the online world. Someone gets nasty, downright vicious, and attacks with cruel knife-to-the-heart words. In RL society, except for the falling-down drunk totally stripped of inhibitions, few would dare to be so merciless. The computer medium sometimes acts like alcohol or drugs in subduing inhibitions, leading to behavior overtly shocking in its raw hostility.

When I first ran across a flamer, I believed such animosity could only come from a lunatic. I soon realized, though, that the "flame" is so commonplace, it could only

Flame wars most often erupt among strangers. New-comers to Internet discussion groups (newbies), and new members of a particular group are often the source of, or the target of, inflammatory messages. Some research findings have suggested that the congruence observed between mood and judgments is due to the current affective mood of the subject taking up memory capacity, leaving less room for consideration of, or attention to, salient details. (Ellis,1991)

The Associative Network Theory model [a set of assumptions that conceptualized the mind and its memory functioning as a systematic network of interlinked nodes] accounts for this in its descriptions of emotional valence as the fundamental way memories are stored. It is a given that when people are presented with a new person or situation, and are called to judge it, they have only their memory of similar events or people to go on. It is apparent then that sad people who read notes from strangers on their computer screens are the ones most primed to make, and act upon, negative judgments of the authors of the messages.

To fully understand the phenomena of flame wars, we must account for the inhibition of normal social norms. The prohibitions against being rude, unkind and argumentative when in a social situation are strong. One of the moderator variables that have been proposed to account for inconsistent findings of congruency in the mood and judgment research is that these effects are not found when such things as established social norms dictate how judgments should be made. (Clark, 1991) be another psychological trait of the human species. A flamer can be a psychopath or Jane Doe in a grumpy mood. Mostly it's the computer medium, like a shot of tequila, that creates the milieu. A happy, content person doesn't usually snap to someone's jugular seeking blood, pain, and death. After stubbing a toe, that same person might be blinded from compassion by inner discomfort. Sometimes, someone reacts to an innocuous post that hits a historic nerve, and a mental toe is stubbed to sudden intense pain.

"Flame wars" start when the attacked party responds to the flamer, usually followed by a free-for-all, barlike brawl. Others jump in and tempers flare. The identification with one side or the other becomes personal as words trigger memories and emotions. Suddenly the stranger attacked by a flamer finds painful memories ignited and passionate anger resurfaces.

> If all computer-mediated communication systems can be said to have one single unifying effect upon human behaviour it is that usage tends to cause the user to become less inhibited. . . . However, being disinhibited is not the same as being uninhibited. MUD players experience a lowering of social inhibitions; they do not experience the annihilation of them. The social environments found on MUDs are not chaotic, or even anarchic. There is indeed no moment on a MUD in which players are not enmeshed within a web of social rules and expectations. (Reid, 1994)

That personal reaction, that hidden hurt that sparks off anger and sends a seemingly nice person off on an emotional kill are special openings into the windows of our inner being. If we could only catch ourselves at it, we'd learn so much. And in strong online communities, people do catch themselves overreacting. They are forced to be introspective and often end up apologizing.

7. Fantasy/Illusion/VR-RL Clash

▶ My first book, *Patpong Sisters*, based on the dissertation I wrote for my doctorate degree in anthropology, detailed mismatched Thai women/Western men pairings. I further attempted to explain such attachments by chronicling my own delusional love affair with a Thai pimp. By observing these inexplicable attachments in other people, I was better able to see them in myself.

The combination of fantasy and reality exists in both VR and RL in varying ratios—this amount of imagination to that amount of fact, sometimes more of one, sometimes more of the other. All human interaction consists of both—obvious in the Thailand pairings, but no less present in a couple married for fifty years. Intellectual creativity defines our species.

Cyberspace arouses my passions, fears, and idiosyncrasies because it connects directly to my inner self. Unexpectedly, what I found online was 100 percent me.

We all have an inner life—the essence of our individuality—that maintains its own existence while it participates with the outer environment. We take inside ourselves what is outside and perceive it through our his-

> From approximately the ninth month of life the child internalizes: he retains as inner objects mental representations of external objects, events, relations, and the feelings associated with these psychological events. Inner objects acquire a relative independence from the correspondent external stimuli that elicited them. They progressively associate and organize in higher constructs. The integration of all these intrapersonal and interpersonal factors gives origin to a potentially infinite psychological universe. (Arieti, 1974: 879)

tory, our personality, and our physiology. While we interpret the world through our historical selves, we also project our inner selves onto the outside.

The characteristics I assign to someone I meet online—a name on the screen—come from within myself. I create the person based on the little bits of input I get from him or her, plus the hoards of associations and emotions within my memory.

On the net, the objective and subjective become enmeshed. From the mouth of a fictional computer geek:

> Objective reality is that which we all share. The sky looks blue, the grass appears the same green, to almost all of us. . . .
>
> But subjective reality is different. Our dreams are subjective reality. There are no rules, no

boundaries, no laws that govern. Virtual reality combines the two, both the subjective and the objective. It creates a new reality where there are no rules. We make the reality whatever we want. We can see it, touch it, feel it, yet it can be experienced by others. (Chapman, 1996:59-60)

> The self refers to the fact that what is objective or objectivizable becomes subjective, is appropriated by the individual as a subjective reality, and becomes part of the individual himself. (Arieti, 1974:896)

In *Patpong Sisters,* I documented numerous Western men involved with Thai women in dual-universe relationships. Each partner's worldview was incomprehensible to the other, and each was lived out in its own orbit. Touching skins did not meld minds. The men tried to make independent yuppies out of the women, who viewed themselves from Buddhist perspectives fashioned by karma and who worried about the day-to-day survival of their poverty-stricken families.

During my research, an American informant named Dudley brought his Thai girlfriend, Sow, to my apartment. I had heard for months about how crazy and obsessed Dudley was with Sow, that he could think of little else. I also knew the story of how they'd met. He'd found her in a bar where all the employees were known to be prostitutes.

"I paid her for sex that first night," he told me, "and for the following months I spent with her. I knew Sow was still working as a prostitute, and when she left me for a week to meet a German customer coming through town, I let her go. It hurts me that she sleeps with other men for money, but I understand her situation. I love her."

I'd also previously met Sow. I'd once visited her bar. After promising not to tell Dudley anything she said, I was able to engage her in a heart-to-heart conversation. I learned that she had two children and not just the one she'd told Dudley about. Her age was quite different from what she'd told him, too.

Even before I saw Dudley and Sow together, I'd been well versed in the infatuations Western men developed for Thai bar girls. The lies the women told the men were not new to me either. However, seeing Dudley and Sow together surprised me with another facet of their relationship—the extent of which I hadn't fully realized—the language barrier. Dudley spoke no Thai and Sow spoke little English. Dudley would say something to me in English, which I translated to Thai for Sow, and then relayed her answer to Dudley.

How, I wondered, could he have such an intense relationship with someone he couldn't communicate with?

My conclusion was that his great love affair existed in his head. Whomever he thought he was in love with was a figment of his imagination. He projected his fantasy relationship onto Sow, often supported by no more than an "I love you" from her. Dudley filled in the verbal gaps with his own desirable dialogue. Her additional

> Men who fall in love with bar girls are entrenched in the ambiguity of never being sure if the women are girl-friends or whores but "the first encounter frequently leads to a quick and intense emotional involvement." (Cohen, 1987:229)
>
> The money she asks for is not represented as payment but as reimbursement for the money she's lost from bar-work and/or support for her family. (Cohen, 1986:115)

statements about needing more money he rationalized or ignored.

Though Dudley knew Sow was a prostitute, he was mostly able to override the facts and doubts and live in his own reconstructed universe.

For three years in Thailand I studied love affairs between Thai prostitutes and Western men. In the following seven years online, I noticed a similarity between cross-cultural affairs and computer romances—the phenomenon of having an intimate relationship that exists mostly in your mind. Seeing a faceless name on your computer screen leads you to fill in the visual blanks with the sexiest, most gorgeous hunk you can think up. In the same way that a daydream can be more pleasing than reality, a real person you meet in the flesh pales next to a cyber lover. The cyber lover possesses all the characteristics, physical and mental, of your ideal mate, with few checks on your imagination.

Although there are plenty of ways to formally meet potential mates on the Internet, most of the people I talked to found their significant others through accident or common interest. Where they found them reads like a guide to the Internet; it seems you can meet people on every part of the Internet. Usenet newsgroups in the "rec" and "alt" hierarchies seem popular, as do music groups. V.J. and Christie met after he posted a message to rec.humor saying his plan file was funny. She . . . sent him mail asking about him, and it went on from there. Other people meet through real time communications. According to Tina, when she and Mark met, "It was one of my first days on the net, and I was still learning the ropes. I had wandered into a channel called #nicecafe, where there [are] a lot of friendly people chatting. He and I started talking, and flirting; the sparks began to fly." (Carlstead)

The three scenarios—cross-cultural romance, like Dudley and Sow's; total cyber romance, like mine with Fire; and in-the-flesh romance, like mine with Jeremy Berg—all point to a similar dynamic. Part of all relationships consists only of what you make of them inside your head.

Trevor has met several VR romantic partners. His illusion of two of them died as soon as he saw them—both being much heavier than they had led him to believe. The weekends of their stays were torture. He acted as gentlemanly as he could while avoiding the amorousness of the relationship they had online.

Trevor's third meeting he called a "setup." He met the woman after he'd posted to a news group. She began emailing him and, eventually, flirting led to them sending email to each other six to eight times a day. When this woman came to meet him, he was not disappointed in her appearance. She was attractive as well as twenty-one years younger than he was. After a short stay in a hotel, she moved into his luxurious house in Miami.

"It didn't feel right," he told me. "From the beginning it didn't feel right. My kids were suspicious of her, too."

She made two trips back to her home in Canada and then told him she wanted to move permanently to Miami. He answered, "Fine. As long as you find your own place to stay."

The affair ended and to this day Trevor has problems because of the credit cards she'd stolen from him after she realized the relationship was not going as planned. One day a strange man, saying he was with the police, tried to extort money from him over her.

Trevor is now wary of online sexual attractions. But does that stop them from happening? No. Though the first three relationships happened years ago, he recently got out of another hot, passionate affair with a married woman. He was so close to meeting her, he'd even had the airplane ticket booked.

Eventually, reason made him question what he was doing, and reason now makes me stop and think, too, when I get obsessed and passionately involved in a computer romance. Nonetheless, it still happens to both of us.

Online, you can be anyone you want and any gender. You can change who you present yourself to be according to mood. Writing about a MUCK (Multi-User Character Kingdom), Benedikt writes:

> My digitized body, curled and pale as my fingers fly across the keyboard to connect to FurryMUCK, stretches and glows as the last letter of the password is entered. Oh, but what mood am I in? The list of my characters beside me includes personalities that in many cases in no way resemble my own. There's "Aileen," a sharp-tongued, stand-offish young woman with a powerful ego and a denial of her own sexuality. There's "Tracey," a forever-sixteen sexpot, blonde and perky, filled with giggles and high school philosophy. There's "Tate," a slender young gay man with soft eyes and a Queen's snappish, flirty disposition. There's "Kari," a young woman discovering her submissive side, nude, and wearing wrist cuffs that advertise her exploration.
>
> In cyberspace, I can become any one of these personas at the tap of a key, like a perfect masquerade. . . .
>
> Within this cyberspace, men and women can in theory take a part of their sexuality and emphasize it without fear of consequences. There is no HIV on FurryMUCK, no herpes, no unwanted preg-

nancies. The physical side of sex is under your control. And this opens doors. I can become this girl Kari, who is slender and young, with golden skin and a winning smile, who wears no clothes, and who sleeps with the stranger who meets her eyes and gruffly orders her to follow him. This drama would never happen in my real life, but in this fiction-world of words I can let my head do it, even my heart, and there's an off-switch by my hand the whole time. (Benedikt, 1994)

In the Living Room on Lambda MOO, I first met Tomato and went off with him to his Tomato Patch. We frolicked in his garden and played with his talking scarecrow. I told him I was twenty-nine. He was thirty-one. Before I knew it, we fell into a lengthy romance and I never quite knew how to tell him I was really forty-five.

The gift of the net is its ability to let us carry fantasy one step further. We all have daydreams and in this space we can act them out with other people. The biggest problem I've seen is when people forget these are two separate realms. The long-lived VR love affairs that disintegrate immediately when the couple meets in person far outnumber the ones that turn into long-lasting RL unions. One Australian MOOer came to the U.S. to meet his love, and for a while they were able to carry on the relationship. They moved in together. They got married. One month later they divorced. "It just didn't work out," Vinny told me on the MOO where he was back in Australia, jobless and depressed.

One day, I found out that my closest MOO friend, Galactica, with whom I'd engaged in hours of girl talk, was in reality a male. This was only slightly disorientating because I knew that on the MOO anything goes. In addition, though, Galactica told me she was a multiple personality and that "they" wanted to come to New York for a weekend to meet me. Of course I wanted to meet her, she was my best friend, and how interesting it seemed! But when I asked her where she was staying and found out that she planned to stay with me—I was filled with foreboding and hurriedly logged off. Aside from being unaccustomed to overnight visitors in my studio apartment, how would I handle some strange guy? Galactica had made it clear that to meet in RL, I wouldn't be dealing with her but with the "core personality," the guy, David. When I mentioned the situation to friends, they answered with words like "mass murderer," "slasher," and "serial rapist."

The situation forced me to face my concept of community. Galactica had been my best friend for months. Here was the test of my sense of connection to MOO society. Whatever the outcome, I needed to prove to myself that I could engage in a trusting relationship.

By evening, I'd calmed down from the panic and was ready to speak to Galactica again. I told her I had only a small room and was busy the Thursday she wanted to arrive. Maybe I could put her up for one night . . . maybe. I wasn't sure I wanted to risk it, no matter what my ideal of MOO citizenship was. Her answer: *We have to talk.* She'd been saying that for days, but I hadn't been paying attention. I then realized she'd wanted to talk ever since "they" had seen the modeling pictures of me on the Web and that David, the core, "had drooled over them."

"Slasher" visions aside, meeting David didn't seem like a good idea, but what could I do. With trepidation, I logged off so that David's call could get through. It turned out he had a great voice. We had an engrossing talk. He was so intelligent! I always knew that Galactica was brilliant and here was confirmation. He even told me his IQ—at the top of the highest one percentile—my kind of guy!

By the end of the evening, and against my better judgment, I agreed to let this strange houseguest, er . . . guests, stay with me. I was unprepared for what happened next—I became obsessed with David.

The fourth day after our phone call, I could think of nothing but David/Galactica. Mentally, I had every sexual fantasy possible with both his male and his female character and even some alternate characters I didn't know.

I fell hard for someone who wasn't even one person. I logged on hoping to speak to David, then realized he wasn't online—only Galactica was there, so I couldn't even have the satisfaction of communicating with my love object.

I had to face the fact that the relationship existed only in my mind. There wasn't even a MOO character to be in love with—just a fantasy in my head with links to a voice on the phone and a female elf on the MOO who described herself as being the green shade of a pool table.

It felt like a zone in my brain had been activated. Although I was sure David was no Mr. Hunky Gorgeous, I was tempted like a teenager with a crush to blurt out, "I'm in love!" The mental switch for "in love" had been turned on and was able to run its course without engagement with the outside world. Like a computer program, it ran full tilt all the way to completion.

My mental construct of this love-of-my-life soul mate vaporized as soon as the real person walked through the door.

"Hi," he said.

"Hi," I answered the RL person, totally disconnecting from his VR image.

He didn't slash me, murder me, or act other than polite. It was my fault that I didn't have an extra bedroom and so woke several times during the night to wild scratching sounds coming from his nylon sleeping bag. The frantic noise signaled that the nearness of orgasm had destroyed his sense of modesty while masturbating.

After David left, he vanished from my life. On the MOO, Galactica and I are still best friends.

Old ideas about "honesty" can't be applied to cyberspace. I learned how differently "lying" was viewed by the Thai culture when I lived in Bangkok. The Eastern concept of "saving face" involved saying things we Westerners would consider lies. To Thais, they were signs of politeness.

Tourists are exasperated by the way Thais on the street send them in the wrong direction when they ask for help finding an address. To avoid "losing face," Thais can't admit to not knowing the answer to a question.

"Truth" is fluid, depending on context and culture. It took me months to learn this lesson doing research on Patpong. My graduate training hadn't prepared me for the

By the time I went to visit I think we were both convinced that it would work out more or less permanently
and we only had to go through the formality of meeting
each other and spending some time together. Well, I hate
to say it, but as soon as I got off the plane and got my
first look it was like a door slamming shut. I'll never forget
that feeling, and never got over the first impression
through the relationship. She was a *lot* bigger than what
I thought she had led me to believe (in good shape,
though). I decided I should try and stay positive, and we
did get along pretty well as friends, but I did tell her about
my reservations. (Albright)

"lying" I encountered during the initial interviews with
Thai prostitutes. I despaired when a woman told me she
had one brother the first time I met her and then the next
time told me she had three.

Different cultures have different methods of expressing personal truth. Likewise, cyberspace has its own
brand. Anyone who's been online awhile knows that a
character named Venus, with flowing red hair and a bikinied hourglass figure, is likely to be a male. This isn't a
lie. It's the freedom of cyberspace. Most longtime MOOers
and Palace members have an opposite-gender "morph,"
an alternate representation of themselves. Why stay a
thirty-four-year-old dumpy male when you have the opportunity to experience being a svelte female, or a moose,

Darth Vader, or the tooth fairy? I have naked male avatars on the Palace for when I feel like being the male in sex, and I have a chick-with-dick one for when I want to really gender-bend.

If its cage door is open, why should the canary stay inside? Fly, bird, fly.

We can't expect to know the reality of the person we meet on the net. Why not accept the leprechaun as a leprechaun? If a relationship continues, it's based on shared interactions that may or may not lead to disclosures and exchanges of photos, a transference of the V relationship into an RL one.

The number of seminude sexy women on the Palace in seductive poses is overwhelming. Some guys get angry at the thought that the beautiful young wench is really an old man. They misunderstand the space. In cyberspace a young girl with cancer can be a princess and a woman so sick with MS that she's contemplating suicide can plan a wedding.

My friend walked into his ten-year-old son's room one night and found him in a role-playing game on a MUD. He was surprised to see his son's name as "Hot Chick" and his description as a *blue-eyed blonde, eighteen years old.*

"Why are you pretending to be a girl?" he asked.

"Because this way everyone wants to play with me. They used to ignore me before."

Makes sense to me.

The times I've been online as a male, I was saddened by the extent to which I was ignored, my greetings unanswered. As a dumb blonde traveling alone through Europe and Asia, I'd never lacked assistance from men.

When I lost a wheel while driving through Milan, a pedestrian who saw me crash into the curb went so far as to offer me his living-room couch to sleep on until my car was repaired. Having a pregnant wife in his bed didn't prevent him from sneaking into the living room in the middle of the night, hoping he'd be paid back for his generosity. Though I disappointed him in that, he continued to let me stay for three weeks until the car was ready.

This same male help is offered to females online. Without seeing a photo or asking my age or appearance, guys rush to answer my questions if I set my @gender to female.

"Gender bending," posing as the opposite gender, is a fact of life in cyberspace. Hopefully, presenting themselves as a female will be an eye-opening experience to men. On the positive side is getting attention, but there are negative sides, too.

Amy S. Bruckman (1995) studied gender swapping on MUDs (Multi-User Domains) and MOOs. She wrote how:

> ... men are often surprised at how they are treated when they log on as a female character. Andrew writes on the newsgroup rec.games. mud:
>
> > Back when I had time for MUD, I, too, played female characters. I found it extraordinarily interesting. It gave me a slightly more concrete understanding of why some women say, "Men suck." It was both amusing and disturbing.

Female characters are often besieged with attention. By typing using the who command, it is possible to get a list of all characters logged on. The page command allows one to talk to people not in the same room. Many male players will get a list of all present, and then page characters with female names. Unwanted attention and sexual advances create an uncomfortable atmosphere for women in MUDs, just as they do in real life.

Carol, an experienced programmer who runs a MUD in Britain, writes on rec.games.mud:

> What I *do* think is funny is this misconception that women can't play MUDs, can't work out puzzles, can't even type "kill monster" without help.

The constant assumption that women need help can be damaging to a woman's sense of self esteem and competence. If people treat you like an incompetent, you may begin to believe it.

More damaging than unwanted sexual advances are unrequested offers of assistance. For this reason many females describe themselves as male or neuter. While males may pose as females to get attention, some females are turned off by the attention. Sexism is also carried into cyberspace by psychologists who continue to use sexist stereotypes that trivialize women when they write about the net. On describing the different types of net addicts, Suler writes:

A teenager who plays hooky from school in order to master the next level of Donkey Kong may be a very different person than the middle aged housewife who spends $500 a month in AOL chat rooms—who in turn may be very different from the businessman who can't tear himself away from his finance programs and continuous Internet access to stock quotes. (Suler, August 1996)

Women in many areas of the computer world (e.g., Borsook, 1996) have run into the gender wall, not only by such portraits of the housewife in a chat room while the businessman uses a finance program, but by men outright blocking them from high-salary computer jobs and by ignoring their very presence in the computer arena.

After finding his ten-year-old son calling himself Hot Chick, my friend was then disturbed to find a disk containing pornography. He could understand the male-and-female-intercourse pictures as something he'd have sought out when he was his son's age. The males having anal sex bothered him, though, revealing a touch of homophobia, and then when he found the GIF of an older man with a fourteen-year-old girl, he became furious.

"How did you get these?" he demanded.

"From a chat board. I was asked what interested me and I made a mistake. I typed a fourteen-year-old when I meant a twenty-four-year-old. Someone sent me this disk in the mail."

My friend called the FBI. They'd seen the photo before and had already apprehended the man responsible for mailing kiddy porn.

Where is the problem? Molestation of children is an assault and harms the child, but the computer is not the villain. When I was ten years old, the elevator man in my building stopped the elevator between floors so he could read me pornography. I had no idea what the words meant, but being held prisoner in the elevator scared me. I was also confused by the school-bus driver, when I was in fifth grade, who insisted on dropping me off last and made me come up front and sit on his hand.

The computer may present a new way to use children sexually, but blame shouldn't be diverted from the real culprits.

8. Community

▶ Virtual spaces are communities, each like a country with its own citizens, rulers, legends, and villains—"geographic" places on our planet with borders, immigration laws, and property rights.

Each society has notions of "proper" demeanor. Online fidelity and cyber adultery is undergoing heated debate. Cybernauts also quarrel over "justice," and when they perceive an authority isn't showing it, they complain. Banishment happens, too, and the ousting of a member is not an infrequent occurrence. Behavior deemed unacceptable or "uncool" results in a person being deleted from the database or banned in all virtual spaces from bbses to CUseeme sites.

Because Echo has been my home base for the past seven years, where I have RL relationships with fellow Echoids, it is to Echo that I bring my troubles. From Echo I acquired my sense of netiquette.

Shame is a major enforcer of community standards. New people learn proper behavior from old-timers. Documents have been written on proper chat netiquette.

COMING ACROSS APPROACHABLY

1) Don't Shout.

Since you can't use bold, underline, or italics on-line and on MUDs, various other ways of emphasizing words have been devised. Marking a word with unusual punctuation, like asterisks or underscores, gives it emphasis (to be read louder or more strongly).

For example: The dog ate my homework!

The *dog* ate my homework!

The dog ate _my_ homework!

The dog >ate< my homework!

Another obvious way to emphasize a word is to put it in all caps. You can easily imagine someone shouting, "THE DOG ATE MY HOMEWORK!" Now imagine someone who always talked that way! "HI GUYS! HOW ARE YOU? I'M DOING GREAT. WHAT ARE WE DOING TONIGHT? ANYTHING FUN?" It makes you want to hold your ears, doesn't it? To come across politely on MUDs, reserve writing in all caps for times when you really mean to be yelling or shouting.

2) Don't Sound Frantic.

Punctuation is plainly an important part of communicating in a text-based medium. How you wield a question mark or exclamation point has more to do with how you come across than you might think!

For example: So, what's going on?

This question sounds pretty laid-back and

calm. But if the person carelessly leaves their finger on the question mark key too long, they'll very likely produce this: So, what's going on?????????
???????????????????????????????????????

Now they sound like they're shouting, frantic, panicked. To come across politely on MUDs, don't overdo your punctuation. An occasional startled "What?!" is okay, but refrain from producing frantic text ("What?!?!?!?!!?!??!?!?!?!?!!") unless you really, really mean it. This amounts to being careful, essentially. Watch what you're typing, and correct mistakes and typos if you make them. (Ciskowski and Benedikt, 1995)

On the Palace, the new guest often arrives speaking in capital letters. *HELLO! ANYBODY HERE SPEAK POR-TUGUESE?*

Kill the cap lock! members are quick to scold. *You're making me deaf!* In most virtual spaces, words in capital letters signify shouting. Juveniles, for some reason, prefer this mode of communicating and often continue it despite others signaling that they are covering their ears and frowning. The pressure to turn off the cap lock is so great that nobody survives long without surrendering to lowercase letters.

When I first became a wizard on the Palace, I grew annoyed at one of the other wizards, mostly because she repeatedly broke the "spam" rule of Echo. She spammed the Palace wizard's "listserv" (an email group with a specific list of subscribers and a specific topic—this one for Palace wizards) with jokes. Spam is any unwanted, unsolicited text that's forced upon you. The longer the message, the greater the annoyance. Copying someone's entire post and then adding one line of comment at the bottom is a serious offense on Echo, though outsiders and usenet newbies do it often. The Palace woman had a habit of doing that and then sending it to the whole list instead of to the one person she was answering. I'd have to wade through screenfuls of something I'd already read to find her silly remark, often just a ROFL (rolling on the floor laughing, another Echo abbreviation taboo). In addition, she spammed the Palace with global messages that only wizards can see. She'd be in a room with another wizard, and instead of whispering privately, she'd use the global page so that every wizard online was subject to her endless joking, often punctuated with a "ROFL."

Aside from the fact that the Palace has two fabulous sounds to indicate amusement, "*)teehee*" and "*)guffaw*," my text-to-speech application pronounced her ROFL as rah-fle, the extended rah sounding like a southern drawl or an English accent. Though I understood she hadn't been exposed to Echo's standards, my annoyance over the rah-fle grew and grew until I couldn't remain long on the Palace before logging off in a foul mood. The woman bugged the shit out of me.

The rah-fler had been my friend before I became a wizard, but irritation over that rah-fle consumed me. I even considered resigning my wizardship.

I wrote about it in Echo's Psychology Conference. It helped when others confessed to having little nonsense things that bugged the shit out of them, too.

Mr. Crane   4-FEB-96 11:11
I go absolutely insane when someone snaps

chewing gum on the subway. Sometimes I get off
the train.

Gloria   4-FEB-96 12:21
    For me it's pen tapping. My boss does this tap
tap tap tap when he's thinking and it makes me
want to pull my hair out.

Choo Choo   4-FEB-96 18:12
    Knuckle cracking. I could scream when I hear
knuckle cracking.

Online communication works well by underscoring
the things we have in common and showing how human
our foibles are. I needed to know I wasn't absurd for being
driven to distraction by the woman's constant use of rah-
fle.

After a few days of whining about it in the Psychology
Conference and receiving supportive answers, I was better able to tolerate the woman. My annoyance went down
by 90 percent.

My overreaction to the woman's ROFLing had disturbed my peace of mind, and before I discussed it on
Echo, I'd found no way to deal with it. As it turned out, a
few weeks later, when I had an emotional crisis on the
Palace, she helped me through it. She proved herself a
good friend and I was thankful that I'd never told her I'd
previously wished her dead. To resolve the residual bad
feelings about her spamming the wizard channel with
global pages, I started spamming, too.

The Sex Conference on Echo has validated issues I'd

been insecure about and informed me of matters of which I'd been ignorant. In the item called "Awful Things Men Do in Bed," I learned a lot.

> *Green Eyes   11-JUN-94 19:11*
> *Don't you hate when you're sleeping peacefully in the morning and all of a sudden that THING is pushing up against you, demanding attention. The guy just needs to go to the bathroom but he insists on waking you up so he doesn't miss the opportunity.*

> *Juniper   11-JUN-94 19:40*
> *I hate that. I wish they'd just go pee. The wetness test also irks me.*

> *Cleo   11-JUN-94 20:10*
> *What's the wetness test?*

> *KZ   11-JUN-94 20:22*
> *You know—when they put their finger in you to see if you're ready.*

> *Cleo   11-JUN-94 20:26*
> *Really? They're just testing to see if you're wet? Damn, I love being fingered. I didn't realize there was an ulterior motive behind it.*

On a MOO, though the programmed atmosphere adds texture, the main appeal is socializing. Each MOO is a community.

I feel a sense of belonging to MOO society, to Echo, to the Palace, to certain areas on CompuServe, and to the

> You sense, even from a brief visit to IRCland, that many of these people have built a kind of community that they would defend as passionately as the most committed WELLite [a member of the Well], habitual mailing-list participant, Usenet veteran, or accomplished MUDder. (Rheingold, 1993)

group of email friends I have in Thailand. Beyond these is a general feeling of belonging to the whole online world. As one virtual space crossed into another, the boundaries between them dissolved. Echoids brought me to the MOO and the Palace; I've introduced my Thailand freinds to the MOO, and when I went to Thailand I took them to the Palace; I've written to strangers after stumbling across their homepages on the Web and have received letters from strangers who saw mine. People on the Well, a San Francisco based bbs, have pointed me to news groups, and after chatting with people on IRC, I've seen them in video with CUseeme. Some of those I exchanged posts with in a news group became email buddies. I've met in person people I originally knew from CompuServe, the Well, MOOs, the Palace, the Web, and email. Cyberspace is a place in its own right, and though we may home-base primarily in one spot or another, overall it's like one country, and we feel citizenship with the other denizens.

A true net addict is a member of several online bbses and has at least one backup Internet service provider, in case of an emergency. The longer people are online, the more virtual spaces they join, so broadening their scope of the net world is a natural progression.

Computerless people listen to my tales of cyber friendships as if I were a child talking about an imaginary playmate. "You went to a MOO wedding last night? Uh . . . um . . . how . . . er . . . interesting."

It needs to be experienced to be comprehended. When I told the receptionist at my office that I spent Sunday in an eighteen-hour marathon writing a MOO program, she smiled as if wondering whether to call for a straitjacket. To me, I'd felt like the sculptor Rodin, lost in eighteen hours of creative trance, a total absorption that blocked out worldly matters.

At age twenty-one, a turned-on hippie product of the 1960s, I left the United States, not searching for anything—just going. After wandering through Europe and the Middle East for three years, I heard about a "freak" community in Goa, India. I'd met a few freaks here and there in my travels. Composed of a variety of nationalities, they were people who'd given up their native lands and their former lifestyles. They had an audacious outlook on life and a collection of utopian ideals. As soon as I arrived on Anjuna Beach in Goa I knew I'd found a home, a community, something to be part of. I felt complete and happy there.

Humans are social beings. We need to aggregate and form bonds. We are dependent on others and are biologically programmed to affiliate. I had a need for community, for belonging, to be part of a family. I didn't know I had that need when I left New York. I left to get away, to disengage. But when I found Goa, I felt a *click*, like a piece of a jigsaw puzzle had snuggled perfectly among matching pieces to form a whole. Finding a home in Goa was the most satisfying thing that had happened to me. It joined me to the universe. I belonged.

I built a house and settled in and planned to live on Anjuna Beach forever. The Goa hippie culture revolved around drugs, though, and wonderful though it was, it couldn't last. After six years I had to leave. I realized that if I didn't, I'd end up in jail for the rest of my life or dead like many of my friends. I left India with a broken heart, sure that I'd never find that sense of home again.

I knew I loved Goa, loved living there, and had felt complete there, but I wasn't aware of how big a part of me it was until I left. I lost my anchor to the world. Afterward, I didn't fit in anywhere.

When I returned to the United States, I enrolled in college. Wow! Learning was as exciting as taking drugs—though I didn't find a community at the school, or anywhere else in New York. I resigned myself to never again "belonging."

Next, I went to Thailand to research prostitution for my anthropology degree. The three years in Bangkok fulfilled my thirst for adventure, but I was as much of a stranger to the Western expat men—who were only interested in Thai bar girls—as I was to the sex workers I studied.

Back in New York, I was still an outsider. My old friends had continued down the consumer/worker path I'd rejected two decades before, and now I had twenty years of exotic experiences that none of them wanted to hear about. To my mother, I was still E.T.

Then I discovered the online world. Online, I found people with a logical style of thinking similar to my own, who were international, logging in from all over the world. Cyberspace was so new, it was like a frontier territory with new laws, rules, and routines evolving day by day. And it was a community, a family. People jumped to offer support, praise, and help with a project. I gloried in being part of that world. When I created a virtual space called Anjuna Beach, Goa, on a MOO, I thought: "Aha, I've come full circle. Home again."

My sense of community formed in Goa. We Goa freaks were bonded by geographic location, the feeling of a small village or a native tribe, something impossible for those raised in a city where you don't know the person in the next-door apartment. The Goa identity brought us kinship with one another—"these are the people I help and go to for help." Though we're now disbanded, spread across the globe, many of us keep in touch and that family feeling still exists.

The net offers the same bond. The place is cyberspace, but the tie of a people related by location is similar. When a Palace member lost her computer after her divorce, others chipped in to buy her a new one so she could stay online even though they'd never met in person. Similarly, I lent a fellow Echoid my laptop when she went into the hospital to give birth, and a group of cyber women threw her a baby show with lavish gifts.

Phiber Optik was a member of Echo who appeared regularly at the Echo f2f bar every other Monday night. When Phiber was arrested for hacking (Slatalla and Quittner, 1995), most of the Echoids were angry and upset, and for the year he was in jail, many made regular trips to visit him. There was an item in the Central Conference devoted entirely to how he was doing, and when he said he needed books, the jail was deluged with so many that friction resulted between Phiber and the jail.

Though hacking is considered a serious crime, to the online world the sympathy for the arrest of a community member overrides concerns about law enforcement.

I know several people from MOOs who've had their homes raided and computer equipment seized. They speak of it as an Englishman would of being knighted by the Queen. Only after I became a Palace wizard did hackers give me cause for worry.

Frank feels deeply commited to his MOO community. He believes the Sex Rooms on Lambda help the citizens to be more honest. "Everyone was having cybersex anyway and now it was out in the open. About 80 percent of guests are really characters. I go into the Sex Room as a guest myself, too. But if I meet someone and it works well, I eventually reveal my character."

Frank had a MOO love relationship when he first joined. It continued for half a year, though he lived in England and she in the United States. They met in person twice. Then the relationship continued on the MOO. "But eventually it just didn't last. The distance between us made it impossible. Now I don't take MOO loves so seriously. I go for the cyber sex but not for a relationship. Sometimes I do get attached to a woman with whom I've

But for a truly convincing glimpse of the high regard in which Phiber Optik is held in some quarters, you'd have to pay an on-line visit to ECHO, the liberal-minded but hardly cyberpunk New York bulletin-board system where Phiber has worked as resident technical maven since last spring. Forsaking the glories of phonephreaking for the workaday pleasures of hooking the system up to the Internet and helping users navigate its intricacies, he moved swiftly into the heart of ECHO's virtual community (which took to referring to him by the name his mother gave him— Mark—as often as by his nom de hack). So that when he was indicted again, this time on federal charges of unauthorized access to phone-company computers and conspiracy to commit further computer crimes, ECHO too was drawn into the nerve-racking drama of his case. . . .

When the news arrived, therefore, of Phiber's 12-month prison sentence . . . it hit like a slap in the face, and ECHO responded with a massive outburst of dismay and sympathy. ECHO's director, Stacy Horn, posted the information at 3 p.m. on November 3 in the system's main conference area, and within 24 hours the place was flooded with over 100 messages offering condolences, advice on penitentiary life, and curses on Judge Stanton. Not all the messages were what you'd want to call articulate ("shit," read the first one in its entirety; quote another: "fuckfuckfuck fuck fuck fuck fuck fuck fuck fuck fuck fuck fuck fuck fuck fuck fuck"), nor was all the advice exactly comforting ("Try not to get killed," a sincere and apparently quite prison-savvy found compatibility. These days everyone has multiple partners and are against MOOnogamy, but in one case I got very jealous and upset when I saw a certain woman with someone else."

I asked Frank if he ever went on as a female guest. "Yes, but I wasn't interested in having sex as a female with a male. I wanted the lesbian sex."

Needless to say, the number of lesbians found in the Sex Rooms is way out of proportion to the numbers found in net society at large.

Over the past year MOO sexuality has evolved, leading us down specific roads. After creating the public Sex Rooms, with doors to lockable private rooms, new rooms were created devoted to sadomasochism and bondage. Frank has traveled this route, too, and now mostly indulges in BDSM (Bondage, Discipline, Sadomasochism) and is a member of a MOO based solely on this style of sexuality.

One day on Lambda, as Olive_Guest, I entered a public room called "School of the Submissive Arts" to find Helix

> Recently, we have witnessed an alarming number of young people who, for a variety of sociological and psychological reasons, have become attached to their computers and are exploiting their potential in a criminal manner. Often, a progression of criminal activity occurs which involves telecommunications fraud (free long distance phone calls), unauthorized access to other computers (whether for profit, fascination, ego, or the intellectual challenge), credit card fraud (cash advances and unauthorized purchases of goods); and then move on to other destructive activities like computer viruses. (Garry M. Jenkins, asstistant director, U.S. Secret Services [Barlow: 1990])

beating Red_Guest with a whip, after having chained her arms to the ceiling. He had whipped her ass, her back, and had been especially brutal to her breasts, which were now covered in welts. They were both naked: Helix standing and Red_Guest dangling from the chains, covered in marks left from the lashing. The following transcript shows the scene as it happened, with others wandering in and out.

SCHOOL OF THE SUBMISSIVE ARTS

This room was created exclusively for the use of Masters and Doms who require a place to train their slaves and submissives. A large four-poster bed is in the center of the room, complete with bedclothes of the softest silk. Leather straps are secured to each post. Feel free to contribute your own special training aids to the inventory here. Helix and Red_Guest are here.

Type "@usage here" for instructions on using this room.

Helix has Red_Guest held securely by her wrists.

Red_Guest leans her head into your chest and kisses. Helix smiles at Red. Red_Guest lifts her eyes and gazes into Helix's with deep trust.

Olive_Guest has arrived.

Helix [to Olive_Guest]: Hello.

Olive_Guest [to Helix]: Hi.

Helix kisses Red's head as he touches her. Helix smiles at Olive_Guest. Red_Guest hangs from the chains, moving gently to the touches of you. Helix looks into Red's eyes as he runs his hands firmly over her body. Red_Guest savors the wondrous touch of you . . . hungry for it!

Helix cups Red's buttocks and pulls her against his hardness, he searches her eyes for the response. Red_Guest's eyes are but a mirror of her body, opening wide to Helix's touch. . . . Her thighs slide open over one of his legs . . . her lips part as if begging for his tongue. Helix presses his lips to Red's and kisses her with passion. Red_Guest welcomes the plundering tongue, making a home for it wherever it might desire to roam. Helix grabs Red's thighs and, reaching under, lifts her legs about his waist. Red_Guest's calves lock behind Helix's hips, her body quakes *with joy as he holds her in his hands. Red_Guest's kisses grow feverish. Helix moans into the kiss, feeling his member throbbing between Red's hot wet thighs. Red_Guest sups upon the moan, her petaled lips press against his member. Helix runs his hand down Red's back and between her buttocks, he presses gently, but surely, a finger against her asshole.*

Red_Guest's tiny opening is true to the rest of her body and, after an initial tightening, opens to his finger . . . no part of her body denied him. Helix looks into Red's eyes as he plunges his finger into her. Red_Guest's eyes widen with the widening of the aperture. . . . She sucks in her breath . . . her belly caves in then relaxes as she welcomes his finger in her asshole. Red_Guest shudders as the probing finger enters the tight passage . . . her hands would be fluttering uncontrollably were they not safely bound. Helix parts his lips and moans gently as he joys in his intrusion. Helix lifts Red gently onto his cock, its head now parting her soaking lips.

Red_Guest's wetness and softness slide over the smooth demanding head. Red_Guest's throat sets up a whimpering of tiny hungry moans as the tender hands place her upon the masculine altar. Helix looks into Red's eyes as he uses his hand with his finger in her ass to hold her firmly as he thrusts. Red_Guest groans deeply. Helix moans, he feels Red clasp his cock within her sweet cunt. Red_Guest clutches with her own legs, her arms' bindings pressing her breasts forward like an offering, her body pinioned by the twin spears of finger and cock.

Red_Guest's inner muscles grasp around the shaft inside . . . and her body sets up a shivering. Helix runs his tongue along Red's welt, ending the line at her left nipple. Red_Guest shifts just slightly, pressing the nipple to Helix's tongue, and her lips whisper a long hissing "yessssssssssss." Helix takes the nipple between his teeth and gently sucks. Red_Guest cries out and arches as the glorious mouth honors her nipple . . . the movement pressing her down deeper on the hand and shaft that support her . . . she clenches her buttocks tightly, feeling the whole hand upon them. Helix thrusts steadily and deeply as he kisses and bites Red's breasts and nipples.

Helix looks into Red's eyes and raises his hand, he thrusts hard and deep as he slaps her left butt cheek. Red_Guest's voice rises from a deep low moan . . . higher and higher with each thrust . . . as her body trembles . . . and her heart soars. Red_Guest groans and slips over into an orgasm of tremendous proportions, the welted left buttock clenching harder under the slaps. Red_Guest groans, "My love." Helix grabs Red's hair and pulls her head back, he runs his teeth down her throat as he raises his hand, once again slapping her tender ass as he thrusts. Helix moans against her sweet neck as he tenses and drives himself deep inside, once again slapping her flesh.

Red_Guest pours her release all over her love's body . . . trembles . . . shudders . . . moans. Red_Guest hears dimly the slap slap of her beloved's hand on her buttucks, reddening beneath his special caress. Helix cups Red's butt and smiles into her eyes as he holds himself deep and hard inside her. Red_Guest gasps and shivers uncontrollably. Helix holds Red's shivering body in his arms.

Red_Guest feels the secondary orgasm loom. Red_Guest clutches her feet round the strong hips . . . and thrusts her own body onto the shaft that impales her. Helix thrusts as he holds Red, his member hard, filling her completely. Red_Guest feels almost as if the tip of her love's cock will appear in her own mouth, so deep does he delve. Helix looks deeply into Red's eyes, he looks at her as he thrusts and slaps her again.

Helix says, "My love, give me your tears."

Red_Guest stares into her love's eyes . . . and growls at him . . . her eyes wet with unshed tears . . . her voice demanding, "Claim me!" Helix pounds into Red again and again as he slaps her soft ass. Helix groans at her demand and grabs her sweet ass between his strong hands.

Ruddy_Guest has arrived.

Rosy_Guest has arrived.

Red_Guest feels the thrusting . . . and the taking . . . the claiming, and releases the last bits of herself. . . . Tears slip down her cheeks and her pussy floods her beloved's shaft so that it glistens and snaps as it pistons inside her. Rosy_Guest teleports out. Helix grabs Red's legs by her ankles and spreads her wide open. Red_Guest cries out as her body swings helplessly, supported only by the wrist bindings and the powerful shaft. Red_Guest wobbles and sways, but the cock holds her steady. Helix moans as he impales Red's exposed and open body, he rams her mercilessly, claiming what is his to claim.

Khaki_Guest has arrived. Khaki_Guest bows.

Red_Guest's head snaps as her body jerks to the thrusts of her beloved. Red_Guest's cries fill the room. Khaki_Guest says, "Uh-oh!" Red_Guest's voice seems to chant a name over and over . . . like a mantra. Helix tenses and arches his back, he wrenches Red open and thrusts hard, exploding deep inside her. Helix thrusts hard and true, impaling Red as she hangs there like a limp soft rag doll.

Red_Guest screams . . . shocked at the sound but unable to stop . . . as the heated gift of her lover fills her body. Helix moans and looks deep into Red's eyes, his final thrusts filling her deep, emptying the last of his load into her soft body. Helix breathes deeply as he folds Red's legs about his waist again, his member grows soft inside her as he presses her head to his chest. Red_Guest's eyes, heavy-lidded and slumberous with sated passion, glue themselves to Helix. She is the picture of satisfied passion. Red_Guest leans her head against the strong chest, beating as passionately as her

own. Red_Guest clings to her beloved completely.
Helix entwines his body with Red's and holds her
tight. Red_Guest gasps into his chest her joyous
satisfaction. Red_Guest murmurs little love
words. Helix has released all the restraints.

Power is as sexy on the net as it is in RL. If wizrocker, the Sprawl God, indulged in all the cyber sex offered him, he'd have calluses as big as marbles on his fingertips. As it is, I hear never-ending reports of females who suddenly fly off to Hawaii (where Rocker and his computer reside).

One of the Palace wizards is a psychologist. He interviewed Jim Bumgardner, the creator of the Palace, on what it was like to be a God.

Well, I think it's probably similar to what celebrities experience (in a much smaller way, since my level of celebrity is proportionally smaller). As of late, I've been noticing that people tend to always laugh at my jokes, even when they're not all that funny. I'd like to think of myself as a funny person, but I can't help but think that people are filtering what I'm saying thru a "jim" filter and therefore reacting more positively to it than they might from others. I've said some things which are quite rude, that folks laugh at, which coming from a Guest might get a rebuke. . . .

Often folks are very genuflective when seeking my advice. "Jim I know you're terribly busy, but I've been waiting for days to ask you this teensy weensy question." (Suler, June 1996)

Over and over on various MOOs, I've heard MOOers complain about wizards with runaway egos who abuse their power. In addition to seeing how that power corrupts, I've observed the hostility that some people have toward authority figures.

Palace members are always clamoring to be wizards, and on one occasion, when God Jim said we needed nominations for new ones, I hinted to a lust object that if he was nice to me, I'd vote for him. Though I made joking reference to "sexual favors," I did indeed want his sexual attention and in my mind it was clearly a "fuck me and I'll promote you" comment. I *)teeheed* and added, *"Uh-oh, now you can sue me for sexual harassment,"* but I was dead serious.

I must have been too subtle or he was too dumbfounded to realize what I meant because he didn't take me up on it. In the end, I didn't nominate him and probably wouldn't have anyway. The event made me realize how easy it is for someone in power to trade gifts for sex.

I'd grown up with sexual harassment as a fact of life. When I was fifteen, I often met men who'd offer me modeling jobs or TV commercials in exchange for sex. I never took them up on it, so I don't know if they would have come through with their side of the deal. The first time I "auditioned" in a fat old man's apartment for a supposed Coca-Cola commercial with The Beatles, it wasn't until he had my pants down and his fingers were exploring that I realized I'd been tricked. Growing up in a rich family hadn't taught me the value of money or of a "job," so I just left in disgust.

While studying prostitution, I empathized with the

poor Thais who faked love and devotion to the moneyed Western men. I didn't realize how easy it was for the men to fall into that sexual power trip until I fell into it myself with wizard privileges to dangle in front of someone I wanted to please me.

For the most part, being a wizard is an act of love. I put in hours every day to keep Harry's Bar fun for members and visitors. To ensure that Guest 681 doesn't go overboard testing how often he could say, "Fuck," I give up time I'd previously used for programming or romancing a cyberbeau.

God Jim possesses tremendous instincts for cyber culture—what holds it together and enchants it. An excerpt from the Palace's Wizard Manual reveals Jim's wit and humor:

CLASSIFYING PALACE ABUSERS

There are a few different types of Palace abusers, not all of them should be killed—some should be gagged, and others simply ignored.

I) "Criminal Psychotics" or "Psychotics": These are users who enjoy annoying others in the worst ways they know how, and will intentionally try to provoke wizards into killing them. Typical quotations:

a) "Suck My Dick" (repeated 100 times by hitting up arrow return)

b) "<insert wizards name here> is a bitch and deserves to die"

c) "Kill Me Kill Me Kill Me"

Psychotics are generally the easiest to identify, and are probably the only case where a killing without warning may be required. However, be careful not to confuse a "child" with a "psychotic." Psychotics will typically attempt to return immediately when killed—see below for how to identify this.

II) "Children": A child is a young user (typically < 15 years old) who delights in the freedoms of the Palace and gets a kick out of seeing the word "fuck" appear on his computer, probably because he is not allowed to use the word at home. Children can easily be confused with "psychotics," but there are important differences. One big difference is that children can usually be "talked down." Typical behaviors for children:

a) Repeating the ")Wind" sound 20 times.

b) Saying "Anyone want to screw?"

A child's level of abuse may vary greatly at different times, depending on the hormone levels. A child's level of abuse may be borderline and may intentionally be just provocative enough to piss you off, but not enough to kick. Such is life. In many cases, it is better to GAG a child (see below) rather than to KILL a child, thus confirming the

Puritan notion that "children are better seen than heard."

III) "Breathers": A breather is someone who continually propositions every user with a remotely feminine name or appearance to have sex, typically (but not always) using private messages. There are two varieties:

IIIa) "Horny Breathers": A horny breather simply wants to have sex. Unlike the psychotic variety, the horny breather will go away when asked. Probably the best thing to do with a horny breather is to tell him to "take it upstairs." Typical quote: "Will you go upstairs with me?"

IIIb) "Psychotic Breather": A psychotic breather specifically is trying to offend and, when greeted by a negative response, will persist even harder. Psychotic breathers tend to be much more obscene and offensive than the milder variety. In some cases, it may be possible to fend off a psychotic breather by acting receptive, but this is probably a crapshoot—a clear-cut psychotic breather should be killed.

Who can say whether there really are psychopaths online or whether the medium "disinhibits" people from social courtesy? There are, however, people online who act abominably. These can be seen from Dibbell's account of a "Rape in Cyberspace," which occurred on Lambda-MOO:

So strong indeed, is the sense of convivial common ground invested in the living room that a cruel mind could hardly imagine a better place in which to stage a violation of Lambda MOO's communal spirit. And there was cruelty enough lurking in the appearance Mr. Bungle presented to the virtual world at the time—he was a fat, oleaginous, Bisquick-faced clown dressed in cum-stained harlequin garb and girdled with a mistletoe-and-hemlock belt whose buckle bore the quaint inscription "KISS ME UNDER THIS, BITCH!" But whether cruelty motivated his choice of crime scene is not among the established facts of the case. It is a fact only that he did choose the living room.

The remaining facts tell us a bit more about the inner world of Mr. Bungle, though only perhaps that it couldn't have been a very comfortable place. They tell us that he commenced his assault entirely unprovoked, at or about 10 P.M. PST. That he began by using his voodoo doll to force one of the room's occupants to sexually service him in a variety of more or less conventional ways. That this victim was Legba, a Haitian trickster spirit of indeterminate gender, brown skinned and wearing an expensive pearl gray suit, top hat, and dark glasses. That Legba heaped vicious imprecations on him all the while and that he was soon ejected bodily from the room. That he hid himself away then in his private chambers somewhere on the mansion grounds and continued the attacks without interruption since the voodoo doll worked just as well at a distance as in proximity. That he turned his attentions now to Starsinger, a rather pointedly nondescript female character, tall, stout, and brown-haired, forcing her into unwanted liaisons with other individuals present in the room, among them Legba, Bakunin (the well-known radical) and Juniper (the squirrel). That his actions grew progressively violent. That he made Legba eat his/her own pubic hair. That he caused Starsinger to violate herself with a piece of kitchen cutlery. That his distant laughter echoed evilly in the living room with every successive outrage. That he could not be stopped until at last someone summoned Zippy, a wise and trusted old-timer who brought with him a gun of near wizardly powers, a gun that didn't kill but enveloped its targets in a cage impermeable even to a voodoo doll's powers. (Dibbell, 1993)

This account of what happened on a MUSH (Multi-User Shared Hallucinations) also deserves mention:

The most striking example of virtual violence that I have come across took place on JennyMUSH. JennyMUSH is a virtual help centre for people who have experienced sexual assault or abuse. Users of this MUSH share a strong bond in their common trauma, and for many of them the MUSH provides their only source of community support. At its happiest, JennyMUSH offers a tremendous example of how MUD programs can be used as valuable social tools. The system was designed with this aim in mind. The chief administrator, or God, of the MUSH is a psychology student whose field of interest is the treatment of survivors of assault and abuse, and the university that she attends fully supports the JennyMUSH project. . . . A single user of JennyMUSH was able to subvert the delicate social balance of the system by using both technical and social means to enact anonymously what amounted to virtual rape. Two weeks after being assigned a character, a user of the system used the MUD's commands to transform him or herself into a virtual manifestation of every other user's fears. This user changed "her" initial virtual gender to male, "his" virtual name to "Daddy," and then used the special "shout" command to send messages to every other user connected to the MUD. He described virtual assaults in graphic and violent terms. At the time at which this began, none of the MUD's administrators, or Wizards, were connected to the system, a fact that may well have been taken into account by the user. For almost half an hour, the user continued to send obscene messages to others. During that time, some of his victims logged out of the system, taking the simplest course to nullify the attack. Those who remained transported their virtual personas to the same locale as that of their attacker.

Many pleaded with him to stop, many threatened him, but they were powerless to prevent his attacks. (Reid, 1994)

The sexual component of cyber life is undeniable and so is the sexual progression we net citizens—the average Joes and Janes—seem to be undergoing. The BDSM trend is too commonplace and out in the open to ignore. In a book called *Grimoire* in the room BDSM Info Center on Strangebrew, the BDSM MOO, are instructions on how to join the community and learn community behavior:

Introduction

This is not, nor is it intended to be, the authoritative text on BDSM in the VR worlds. It was intended, originally, as an essay, for publication on the Web, and as such, has several references to real life play; I left them in. This is not the "last word" in BDSM, just one Dom's opinions. . . .

What is BDSM?

The title, BDSM is a sort of catchall phrase for a large group of sensual diversions, the letters stand for Bondage, Discipline, Sado (Sadism), Masochism. Basically, it is all best described in terms of Domination and Submission. One person, dominating another, physically, emotionally, and/or mentally with the full consent of the one submitting. BDSM is not about rape or abuse—it is, in its truest sense, an exchange of power, between willing partners, for the mutual satisfaction of each other's needs.

Domination:

While most Doms affect a stern and even cold outward demeanor, good Dominants are highly empathetic, being able to anticipate and build on the feelings and emotions of the Submissive. To draw those feelings and sensations from their partners, like a Virtuoso draws forth music from a violin. The best Doms thus have an instinctive understanding of the human psyche.

Submission:

It has been my experience, that the best Submissives are strong, confident, and highly intelligent people. This may sound incongruous, but submission is not at all about being a doormat. The Sub relinquishes control, thus freeing themselves of the normal constraints of everyday life, liberating the id, so to speak, gaining the freedom to just feel, and simply experience sensation is the rush that many seek. My Sub describes it as a freedom from choice, from having to make decisions, because all the relevant decisions are being made by someone she trusts.

Bondage:

The art of restraint: physically limiting the movements of the submissive, seems to have the effect of heightening sensation. For me, I do get a charge out of knowing that the Sub is helpless, and completely under my control. It also allows the sub to struggle, without detracting from what you are wanting to do. Whether one uses silk scarves, clothesline, ropes, straps, duct tape, or expensive and exotic leather bindings, the result is the same. A note of caution, play safe, never, I repeat NEVER leave a person restrained and unattended.

The tract goes on to include Taboos and Limits and offers advice on meeting the right partner.

In another book in the room BDSM Info Center, community standards are described for the MOOers, such as:

-BDSM FAQ-

This section regards standard greetings between subs and doms. There are a number of viewpoints on this subject, and this is not meant to be prescriptive. You may notice that some players lower their eyes, or "cast" to others. If you are a submissive and wish to emulate this practice, there are three basic approaches. First, you can elect to "cast" only to your own dom, if he or she desires it. Second, you can choose to "cast" to your dom and those players for whom you have a particular desire to. Third, you can follow the "if it moves, cast to it" approach, as follows:

Q: When and how to cast your eyes down?
A: A slave or submissive has to cast his/her eyes down when,

—He or she enters a room where one or more masters/mistresses are.

—A master/mistress enters the room where the sub/slave is.

How to cast has been made easier by Mystery (thanks for it).

1: Add the feature by typing @addfeature #2313
2: On this feature, multiple verbs are written but the cast verbs are to be used as followed.

@cast <player>—just like "cast," more or less.

@cast—cast your eyes down in general, not to any single person.

@cast <player> <player> <player> etc.—cast to a group at once.

@cast all—cast your eyes down to everyone in the room who either

(1) is listed as a dom on the subclub roster, or

(2) has a @master-ed slave.

Who knows if this is just a passing phase? Who knows where delving into our sexual fantasies may lead us as RL people?

Helix, after I met him in his interaction with Red_Guest, became a MOO friend of mine with whom I've discussed this trend. He noted:

"Another woman I know had been raped a few times when she was very young and in her teens as well. Now she wanted to reenact the rapes online through playing on MOO. She wanted to relive these encounters and did so twice with me. It must have been like a cartharsis with her and a self-examination of what these events had done to her and her thinking about herself. She was looking for some answers. It made her hot, but there was something else that she was processing in all of it. I called her once after an encounter and she was in quite a state and we talked a bit. It lasted only a few weeks, but I figure you can't have a meaningful long-term relationship with someone who has raped you even in VR and even just for the purposes of reenactment. Again I have no idea whether this helped or hindered her. The only thing I know for sure is that she was dealing with her stuff and that was one of the ways she went about doing that."

Like dreams, cyberspace is a mingling of things and relationships that we hold within ourselves, the same ingredients but cooked up in a different kind of oven. Sexuality has its own nook in our brains. While it has ties to other emotional responses, it has a distinct quality of its own, unconnected to anything except itself. This can be seen most clearly in fetishes—arousal by a foot, a shoe, or some strange object. Like the imprinting for "mother," whereby hatchling ducks will follow any mechanic/organic moving thing seen during the short time span in which they are in the imprinting stage (Lorenz:1952), human sexual bents are similarly imprinted. A type of person, an object, a sexual practice gets coded into our sexuality chip and stays there.

Cyberspace is my adopted community. I'm connected, and not just to a set of blood-related relatives I may or may not like as people, but to chosen kin. The global span of the net may break down the barriers that created clan wars, religious wars, and national wars. Though we do feel compelled to fight to the death in the Mac versus PC war, we can also laugh at ourselves for doing so.

Cyberspace may bring about a new world order. It's here. It's new. It's revolutionizing old concepts and from it will come an upheaval of social change. Some may deny it, but the net phenomenon sweeping the globe is real.

On July 9, 1996, a Palace global page called us to the wizard's study.

When I arrived, Blondie said, *Robin died today with the help of Dr. Kevorkian.*

Oh! I answered, stunned. After a few seconds I wrote, *She'd told me she planned to commit suicide. I had no idea she was going with Kevorkian. Or that it was even true.*

Blondie continued, *She's been telling me how bad her multiple sclerosis had become, and that she wanted to die. She gave me the date, today, but she never mentioned Kevorkian. I just heard it on TV. I know it's her.*

Saintj asked, *Are you sure it's Robin? Do we know her real name?*

I said, *I feel so sad. I know she was plagued with guilt about sin but she very much wanted to die.*

Blondie said, *We should plan a moment of silence for her.*

Saintj said, *Yes. Or a memorial service where we speak about her. Then we can send the log to her daughters.*

I said, *I wonder if I should write to Dakota about it.*

Even though I knew how real online people were, I was still shocked when the R world collided with the V world. I turned to CNN and soon heard news of Dr. Kevorkian's latest assist, his thirty-third. They said Robin's real name—Rebecca Badger.

KEVORKIAN ASSISTS IN HIS 33RD SUICIDE

DETROIT—Dr. Jack Kevorkian helped a 39-year-old woman with multiple sclerosis commit suicide with a drug injection, then took the body to a hospital himself, confident that the "era of harassment and persecution is over" for him.

It was the 33rd suicide in which Kevorkian has taken part since 1990 and the fifth since his most recent court victory, on May 14.

Kevorkian and another doctor took the body of Rebecca Badger of Goleta, Calif., to Pontiac Osteopathic Hospital Tuesday, Kevorkian's attorney, Geoffrey Fieger, said. Fieger refused to give details.—The Associated Press

The collision of media was confusing and jarring—Robin my Palace friend and Rebecca Badger from TV. My relationship to Robin and to Dakota and the memories from the aborted wedding confused me, too. We'd been wrapped up in each other's real lives—more than any of us knew. Our three fates had flowed together and gotten tangled in the river of cyberspace.

Now, five months later, a real personality and her reality came at me from a report on TV. In *Twilight Zone* fashion, we'd been on separate plains of existence while on a shared one. I wrote to Dakota.

The next day he answered. *I am crying. Robin had been the light for me that made the candle glow.*

I wanted to write something about Robin on Echo. Echo has items for noting what happened in our daily lives. I wrote:

I am sad.

> *The Kevorkian woman today was a longtime Palace member. She was very sick from MS. She went blind a few weeks ago. She really wanted to die and couldn't take the pain of living anymore. I didn't know she was doing it with Dr. Kevorkian. Just found that out tonight. Her daughter was with her at the time.*

> *Bye, Robin.*

In the Web Conference, under the item "The Palace," I wrote: *Palace member Robin died yesterday with the help of Dr. Kevorkian. We are planning a memorial service. I'll post the details as soon as I know them.*

A partial transcript of the Palace log from Robin's memorial service:

> **** Robin's Memorial will be starting in a few minutes . . . please proceed to Heaven's Gate.*
>
> *River: And please maintain silence during the reading of the poems.*
>
> *Nitehunter: I'm trying to get a halo.*
>
> *Vindicator: Anybody want this prop of animated teardrops?*

BamaBelle: I want the teardrops, Vin. I'm crying in real life, too.

Vindicator: Bama, they are numbered. Which ones are you missing?

BamaBelle: I have 1 2 3.

Vindicator: That's all of them. Three teardrops to run down your cheek.

BamaBelle: Did someone get in touch with Dakota?

Cleo: I did, Bama.

BamaBelle: Is he coming? He should be here.

Blondie: Dakota is out of town.

Cleo: I haven't heard back from the last email.

MsDream: Dakota broke her heart, what can he do now?

Blondie: Please don't pass judgment here. Very few know all the details.

*** *Last Call to Heaven's Gate for Robin's Memorial. We are about to start.*

*** *We are here today to Honor Robin, a dear friend of ours from the Palace.*

*** *I am going to read a few poems, then we would like you to say a few words. We will be taking a screen capture. The logs and pictures will be sent to Robin's daughters.*

*** *Ultimate Eternity, Dedicated to Robin by Palace member DieHard* (Aron Buchholz)

I hear the crystal echoes of sweet angels' voices
they call from the crashing waves
and teach my heart the rhythm of the sea
This is where my world becomes real
for this is where I belong
I am called home from my long journey
to my final resting place amid the clouds

I am home within my deep seclusion
trapped in the minds of those who loved me
and at peace
I have become the ultimate eternity

*** Please bow your heads for a moment of silence before we begin sharing.

Eyebrow: Wow!

Blondie: Bama? You knew her well.

BamaBelle: Robin, I will miss you very much. You told me you would be my angel and now you will. I love you and I'll miss you a lot.

Kaitlyn: It was nice to see her face each time I came into the gate at Main.

MsDream: God bless you and keep you, Robin.

Blondie: I knew Robin for months and she never complained . . . what an upbeat and wonderful person she was.

Natasha: I didn't know Robin . . . I know of suffering. . . . She chose her path to peace and she rests.

Blue Knight: She now knows the great unknown, that which we all will one day know. Rest in peace, dear one.

Cleo: Good-bye, my friend Robin. You have enriched my life by knowing you. You have enriched cyberspace by showing us how real are the people behind the props. You have strengthened our Palace community by binding us in the reality of the love we feel now for our member Robin. Thank you for spending some of your last days with us. Your presence in my cyber life was a gift.

Jeannie: Robin, I miss U dearly. U will always be deeply loved here. So many times I would see her laughing in the bar and talking. She would always make me laugh.

L.A.: Robin was always there for me. . . . We would talk about what was happening in each other's lives. Now I'll be there for her, forever, in my heart.

Spock: She was very brave to make the decision she did.

Suffering proves nothing, except to extend the anguish of those you love.

Blue Knight: Amen.

Buggie: Very brave.

River: Robin, I just want you to know I enjoyed knowing you and will miss you always.

*** Are there any last words before we once again bow our heads?

Jessica: I didn't even know you, but I wish I did. I feel for all and it looks like everyone looked up to you. I hope you rest in peace.

MsDream: Good-bye Robin—till we meet again.

*** In Robin's Memory . . . A new Room is being built and added. It will be called Robin's Garden.

Jeannie: :(

tds: You have left your memories with us, Robin.

Jason: You are wonderful caring people here at the Palace! This is nice but sad!

*** Thank you all for coming to share your hearts. We love you, Robin.

A few days later, an article in *The Washington Post* reported that Robin had been wearing a Palace T-shirt when she died.

9. Consequences?

Censorship of the net is a nontopic. The horse has escaped; no use trying to close the barn door. The horse has been gone so long, it's mated and produced new generations and no one can possibly get all those horses back in the barn now.

Cyber sex as a phenomenon is here, and short of closing down the net, there's no way to stop it. The birth-control pill started the sexual revolution because it freed women from unwanted pregnancy. The net will now free women from the consequences of societal stigma. They will be able to express their sexuality among other people, instead of masturbating alone in the dark.

Anonymous orgies, VR romances, encounters that lead to short RL affairs are only some facets of online sex. An experimental, sexual romp can develop into a long-lasting RL union.

Within my first few months of MOOing, I fell into a three-month MOOnogamous relationship with a man who was into sadomasochism.

Though I was anxious about entering the dangerous-sounding love affair with a man whose description re-

> The people of medieval Europe had twelve generations during which to adjust to the idea that women were worthy of respect, the Victorians three generations to accept that they were worthy of the vote. The modern world has tried to adapt to the idea of almost complete legal and sexual equality in a couple of decades. . . .
>
> Because the first and most revolutionary aspect of woman's liberation was her new sense of sexual independence, humanity's 5,000-year-old instincts sustained a sudden and severe shock. In reality, much of the frenetic sexual activity that appeared to ensue was an illusion fostered by the fact that journalists and media personalities began writing and talking about sex with unheard-of frankness (and, indeed, seemed to write and talk about nothing else), but even this was enough to set the less liberated off on heated tirades about "declining moral standards." All that they were really complaining about, if only they had recognized it, was that some women had begun doing what most men had been doing since the beginning of recorded history—sleeping around. (Tannahill, 1992:423)

vealed him to be carrying assorted dildos and handcuffs, I couldn't deny that I also found it titillating. Though I feared that I'd find out I actually leaned toward perversity, I decided to enjoy the fantasies. In doing so, I discovered there was an end to my curiosity. When I reached it, I was uninterested in going further. I was glad to find out that I wasn't really bent on S&M. The boyfriend wanted to meet me in RL, but I never intended to try that out on my real flesh. The thought of meeting him in person was a turnoff. As a fantasy, I enjoyed it immensely, but that was enough. Sexologists have long noted that it's normal to fantasize about sex with a TV star or the plumber while engaged in the act with a spouse. If it adds to your pleasure, it's harmless. Similarly, though I've grown to love sucking cock on the MOO, in a recent bout of RL lovemaking, I found myself thinking: "Ugh, when will it be polite enough to stop doing this?" What I craved on the MOO had not crossed over into RL.

The Internet is a wonderful tool for trying on behaviors and personalities and escaping on wild adventures without having to actually live them. I learned that there's a distinction between fantasy acts and acts I'd really perform. This was an important lesson. Beforehand, I never knew for sure whether I wanted to live out my daydreams. Now I know the answer—I don't.

Denise is a "slave" on the MOO, but she told me: *I'd never do this S&M stuff in RL, but here it's a turn-on. In RL, I'm quite a control freak, and the funny thing is, I think some of these "master" guys here are wimps in RL. They seem to have a lot of anger and frustration in their RLs. But if they want to take it out on me here, why not? I enjoy it.*

Judy is a Palace dominatrix. She has rooms with bondage GIFs, portraying assorted torture devices. She told me, *The guys come back and back. They want to be beaten and have things put up their ass. It's hot for me, too, but, no, there's never been one I've been romantically involved with, though they shower me with adoring statements. And I'd never meet one of them in RL.*

The MOO offers other ways to release frustrations and attain revenge. Sometimes I listen to Rush Limbaugh on the radio because he's funny. His sexist attitude toward women, though, taps my poor-me-the-pitiful-female monster and heightens the powerlessness associated with it. I'm unable to change the status of women in the world or in my own country. To pacify the monster, I made Rush Limbaugh the host of the Patpong Bar in an "enterfunction" program that runs whenever someone—for example, Orange_Guest—enters the bar. *Rush Limbaugh says, "Greetings, Orange_Guest."*

Visitors who notice that no live characters are present would be tempted to type *look rush* to view his description: *A large talkative man who is groping Nok the Prostitute.*

After a ten second pause: *Rush Limbaugh [to Orange_Guest]: Please type "ditto Rush."* Fans of the real Rush Limbaugh are called "ditto heads" because when they call in to his radio show, they show support of his views by starting their phone conversation with "Ditto, Rush." When the person responds with *ditto Rush*, my program goes into effect:

Orange_Guest says, "Mega dittos Rush!" Rush Limbaugh says, "Hello, Orange_Guest. Try one of the prostitutes here. They have talent on loan from God. I know. I've tried them all." Rush Limbaugh [to Orange_Guest]:

"Drink a Patpong Snapple. Delicious. Shine the light of Patpong on America. Type: 'order Patpong Snapple.'"

Heeheehee, my MOO skills have granted me control over Rush Limbaugh.

Before Rush responds to *ditto*, the program checks for gender. If the player who activated him is female, Rush adds: *You must be a Feminazi because they are the only females smart enough to MOO.*

Sexism exists on the net as it does it RL, but perhaps this will change as more men experience being a female character. After a year or so on the net, I found myself becoming more aggressive. I don't know if it was related to computer life, but it's possible. I'd conquered the computer enough so that when I encountered sexism, which happened often, I fought back because I had the means to do so. And not just in cyberspace. When the organization I worked for wanted a Web page, I offered to help the computer department in my office. I had the skills to do it, but my offers went ignored. Finally I bypassed the men and went to the company president. Then I became Webmaster.

Not long after attaining my position as Webmaster, I was dismayed to receive a note from the Mensa Webmaster saying he had removed my link to their list of Mensan homepages because of its content. He said my Razor Blade Show lacked taste. I was hurt by the rejection and incensed that one man could censor my presence as a member of Mensa. I fought back, creating a "Mensa Censors" Web page, which resulted in a furious debate between Mensans, Webmasters, and strangers, which lasted months. Previously, direct confrontation had never been

> Tasks and roles assigned to men and women in our own cultural tradition were assumed to be correlated highly with anatomically based aptitudes. . . . In the era between the late 1930s and the mid-1960s this notion was challenged. . . . Cross-cultural data on the sexual division of labor very quickly dispelled the idea that men (or women) are unable to do some of the tasks assigned women (or men) in our culture. (Leibowitz, 1975)

my style. Maybe maturity brought the change; maybe competence. Or maybe the safety of the virtual world made it possible.

My old dumb-blonde image must have followed me to the net with the picture I put on the homepage, encouraging the Mensa Webmaster to think he could so easily oust me. To protest and retaliate, I employed technological skills, plus psychological ones gained from observing the dynamics of online interaction. To ride the tide of outrage that had recently swept the net over censorship, I used the free-speech, blue-ribbon GIF, which resulted in angry letters sent to my opponent and cc'ed to me. The Mensa Webmaster never did reconnect me, but the fuss and the new friends I acquired were even better than being one link among hundreds on the Mensa page.

I am definitely more prone to aggression, vindictiveness, revenge, and retaliation online than off. When some-

> A male respondent reported that his computer was male ("my mate Micky"), but, he said, "I always refer to my dual disk-drive as female — she's lovely" (Shotton 1989, 194-195). Notice: his active, powerful, intelligent, logical computer was male like him, while his obedient, passive, receptive disk-drive was female. (Holland, 1996)

one's feelings are involved, I've learned to temper the mean responses, though. Since Robin's death, I try to think before I write an angry message because I'm more aware that there is a real person at the other end. Still, the boldness at expressing anger frees me.

Are children exposed to sex on the net?

To answer the question: "Who is using the net?" demographics are provided by http://www.cyberatlas.com/demographics.html.

> One of the most popular questions we receive pertains to the industry activity and professional characteristics of Internet users. In terms of industry activity, a partial answer is provided by the CommerceNet/Nielsen Internet Recontact Survey. . . .

DEMOGRAPHIC PROFILE
OF INTERNET USERS

Academic Users 15%

Recreational Consumers 27%

Corporate Users 46%

Occupational Consumers 12%

According to Nielsen Media Research, 64 percent have at least a college degree, which reflects the influence of academia on the Internet. . . .

A consensus of various studies indicates that 32 percent of Internet users are female. . . .

About 73 percent of Web users are from the U.S., 11 percent hail from Europe, and 8 percent from Canada and Mexico. . . .

Studies that delve into the motivational behavior of Web users show that 70 percent of the Internet population is made up of "actualizers" and "experiencers." These groups lead social change and gravitate toward parts of society associated with innovation—universities, trendy city neighborhoods, fashionable occupations, etc. . . .

GVU5 reports that 87 percent of respondents are white. FIND/SVP says that 5 percent of Internet users are African-American, 3 percent Hispanic and 3 percent Asian.

The average age of computer users is 39, while the average Internet user's age is 32. About one in 10 Internet users (more than 3 million) is a child under 18 who uses the Internet from home or school.

Aside from the pedophiles who specifically seek them, adults would be quick to disconnect from minors due to moral beliefs, disinterest, and especially boredom. Immaturity is a handicap in cyberspace. However, children are undoubtedly there. For several years Echo took part in the New Year's Eve celebration at Grand Central, offering worldwide chat via ten computers on the balcony of the gigantic marble train station while hundreds of people waltzed to a full orchestra below. Some Echoids stood by to offer a keyboard to passing revelers. I found it impossible to pry off a computer a handful of thirteen- to fifteen-years-olds. They would not budge, despite the crowd of people waiting a turn.

Minors are online. They love to chat and are experienced at it.

Who can guess at the repercussions of coming-of-age while playing in a MOO Sex Room? With so many variables—changing gender, role-playing, self-awareness—it could be decades before a psychological study can gauge long-term effects.

I imagine that when telephones first came into widespread usage, people thought they could live without one in their home or that they could control their children's access to it.

Cyberspace will be no less insidious or revolutionary than the telephone.

After a MOO relationship where I net-sexed every day for months, the thrill wore off, and with it, the attraction to

The industry itself said that telephone calls enriched social ties, offering "gaiety, solace, and security," even making of America "a nation of neighbors." Less interested parties, as well, described the telephone as a device that worked on behalf of social attachment. The most common claims were that the telephone allowed rural people to overcome isolation, perhaps even saving many farm wives from insanity. Others, however, charge that the telephone provides but an echo of true human communication. . . .

A second and widespread conviction is that telephone use weakens local ties in favor of extralocal contacts and national interests. Some make this claim approvingly, stating that the telephone is "an antidote to provincialism." Increased communication promises to advance contact among cultures, to help bring "the brotherhood of man." But for others the telephone is yet another of modernity's blows against local *Gemeinshaft,* the close community. We get larger "electronic neighborhoods . . . but shallower kinds of community." Ron Westrum has argued that devices such as the telephone "allow the destruction of community because they encourage far-flung operations and far-flung relationships." At an even deeper level the telephone contributes to placelessness, and without rootedness both community and identity are at risk. (Fischer, 1992:24-25) my cyber lover. The urge to slut around also died and I was no longer falling in love with any old intriguing name on the screen. I thought I'd become jaded. In the fall of 1996, Echo crashed and I couldn't use my PPP connection. All I could do was telnet from the Well, and after a few hours on Lambda as a guest in the Sex Room, I got caught up in it once more and spent the next few days glued to my keyboard. After a two-and-a-half-year hiatus from MOO relationships, I found myself involved with Calculus, creating a sex haven for ourselves on another MOO. Once again I became obsessed with a cyber lover. This experience convinced me that the powerful draw of MOO sex obsession doesn't fade with time. It's too compelling.

Net sex had changed in the time I'd been away from the MOO, wizzing the Palace. It had taken on a characteristic of MUDs—role-playing. People would set up a scenario, describe what happened before *(I kidnapped you off the street)*, where they were *(We are in an underground bunker. You are lying tied up and blindfolded)*, and would act out the sexual fantasy. Two people, locked in a room, carried out their roles, and when they wanted to step out of character they'd send a page, even though there were only two of them in the room. The page signaled a stepping out of the scene and could be used for *Do you like this?* or *Tell me when you are close to coming.*

In those few days I tried out dozens of partners, both characters and guests, and everyone was using this new style. This was when I discovered that the art of MOO sex had evolved, and the S&M factor had taken over many of the Sex Rooms. All were now programmed for bondage and many of the characters and guests had added words like "submissive" or "dom" to their descriptions.

People programmed sex toys that could be used on others. For instance, Helix made a bullwhip with various verbs. With simple commands, Helix would receive one message and Red_Guest another as he used the whip on her. An observer in the room would receive a separate message, describing what Helix was doing to Red_Guest. Some examples are (the "you" being either Helix or Red_Guest who was the target):

> *(Helix sees) You uncoil the bullwhip and snap it at Red_Guest.*
> *(Red_Guest sees) Helix uncoils a bullwhip and snaps it at you.*
> *You yelp in pain as the bullwhip hits your skin and leaves a small red welt behind.*
> *(Helix sees) You uncoil the bullwhip and snap it at Red_Guest. You use the bullwhip to pull Red_Guest to you and kiss her passionately.*
> *(Red_Guest sees) Helix uncoils a bullwhip and snaps it at you. The bullwhip wraps around you and Helix pulls you into his arms and kisses you deeply on the mouth.*
> *(Helix sees) You pull back the bullwhip and snap the air. CRACK!*
> *(Red_Guest sees) Helix uncoils a bullwhip and snaps it at you.*
> *You jump back as the bullwhip cracks the air in front of you.*

The sadomasochistic aspect of MOO sex is still a puzzlement. Earlier, when I'd been working on Nok the Prostitute, a MOO friend was fashioning a "Justine" bot, modeled after de Sade's *Justine* (1791), a book full of beatings and rape.

Some definitions of sadomasochism don't describe at all what is happening on the MOO: "Sadomasochism may be operationally defined as obtaining sexual arousal through receiving or giving physical pain." (Gebhard, 1979:162) A MOO whip does not hurt RL skin. Another part of the report, though, may hint at why it is so popular on the MOO.

> This pre-coital activity has definite neurophysiological value in establishing or reinforcing many of the physiological concomitants of sexual arousal such as increased pulse and blood pressure, hyperventilation, and muscular tension. . . . This may explain why sadomasochism is used as a crutch by aging men in our society who require some extra impetus to achieve arousal. (Gebhard, 163)

When I've questioned other MOOers why it was so prevalent, a frequent answer was that it provided that extra little boost to arousal. All the Lambda Sex Rooms are preprogrammed for bondage. When you enter the room, you receive the message: *Type "@usage here" for instructions on using this room.* Typing @usage here gives the message:

To fasten a player securely in the restraints on the four-poster bed, type the following:

> *restrain <player> in wrist_straps*
>
> *restrain <player> in ankle_straps*

To fasten a player to one of the chains hanging from the ceiling:

> *chain <player> at <player's body part>*

To release your captive, type the following (only the player who fastened the restraints can release them using this command):

> *release wrist_restraints*
>
> *release ankle_restraints*
>
> *release chains*

****** PANIC RELEASE INSTRUCTIONS ******

If you need to get free, type @release, panic_button, or safe_word. This releases all the restraints in the room and sets all related properties to 0.

If Green_Guest typed *restrain Olive_Guest in wrist_straps* and *restrain Olive_Guest in ankle_straps*, the screen would say: *Green_Guest fastens the leather wrist restraints to Olive_Guest's wrists, spreading Olive_Guest's arms out wide across the four-poster bed. Green_Guest fastens the leather ankle restraints to Olive_Guest's ankles, spreading Olive_Guest's legs out wide across the four-poster bed.*

Or if Green_Guest typed *chain Olive_Guest at arms,* the screen would say: *Green_Guest fastens Olive_Guest to chains suspended from the ceiling, attaching the chain's leather and steel fasteners firmly to her arms.*

I've played the role of master, going to someone's room after seeing him slinking around the Dungeon, averting his eyes. I tied him in wrist and ankle restraints. I called him names and smacked him with virtual toys. It was interesting but also a lot of work.

In December 1996, the Internet made the headlines and television news when a woman accused a man she met in an America Online chat room of sexually torturing her. At first glance, a description of what happened sounds similar to what happens in a MOO Sex Room:

> Jovanic, who had allegedly prepared for the evening by pre-cutting strips of cloth and a blindfold, allegedly began tying up the student in a playful way.
>
> She protested, but by then it was too late: she was trapped.
>
> Jovanic allegedly completed tying up the student, stripped her of her clothes and dripped hot candle wax all over her body.
>
> He also allegedly bit the woman's breasts, molested her with a baton and made repeated references to sicko serial killer Jeffrey Dahmer, who dismembered his victims and saved some of their body parts. (Pearl and Francescani, 1996:4)

What needs to be remembered is that psychopaths existed before the Internet and would likely act the same way with someone they met at a bus stop. The man was a Columbia University doctoral student, someone a mother would be eager to have date her daughter and who would be afforded trust by many. Jovanic was planning to see, in person, others he'd met online, too.

I'd seen a show in a Patpong bar where a man poured hot wax on himself in a provocative manner. These things exist outside of cyberspace. A later report noted that Jovanic's ex-girlfriend had also accused him of terrorizing her. She'd met him at their university, not on the net.

Return to Reality

When my job sent me to a conference in Thailand for one week in 1996, I jumped at the chance to see my old friends, both Thai and Westerners. I didn't expect to have reality thrown in my face like a glass of iced oolong tea.

All the emotions I'd seen inside myself from CPU vision hit me—only this time brought on by real-life people in real-life events. First came lust. On arrival in Bangkok, I had a sexual tryst with a Western friend. We had plain old vanilla intercourse. Not one thought of any kinky thing I'd done on the MOO entered my mind. My RL sexual response was the same as it had always been, though perhaps I was more sympathetic with, and attentive to, my partner's sex organ. Having had a penis of my own online made me more conscious of his.

The sexual union was fabulous and great fun, but I wasn't interested in establishing a relationship with the guy. He wasn't my type despite the sexual attraction. Nonetheless, my romantic node geared up without my consent. And so came jealousy and the other obsessive parts of myself I'd been made aware of by the computer

I became angry the next day when he didn't return my call, as upset as I'd been when Jagwire had sent me a mispage or when Fur didn't beg me into his Palace site or when Dakota announced his wedding. I felt slighted, unfairly treated, ignored. I didn't want him yet went berserk at the thought that maybe he didn't want me. What was the feeling? Loss? Abandonment? He never actually said he didn't like me. The rejection scenario took place in my head. Our sexual bout should have been a simple holiday hoot, but the wrong buttons got pushed in my brain. My original plan had been to seduce him and then forget it, something I'd done often, which was usually followed by the guy eager for more. But this guy wasn't and so came an avalanche of linked emotions. They arrived as reactions to a situation that didn't exist in the present but in the past, maybe the original rejection from my mother. It took about a week to recover from Jagwire's mispage and Fur's disinterest, and this, too, would have faded were it not for the onslaught of additional bad feelings.

Next, during that reality break in Thailand, came the sexual-envy monster. It returned me to the state of mind I'd been in during my years of Patpong research when I studied Western men gaga over illiterate, unsophisticated, poor Thai women. The men found the submissive Thais more satisfying than women of their home countries, and they gave up everything to live permanently in Thailand. The memories and their connected feelings grew from inside my head. I longed to log on to the Palace and kill a few obnoxious guests. Maybe that could have helped center me; or if I'd been able to post about how I felt in the Psychology Conference on Echo, others would have offered support. The virtual community would have been behind me as I dealt with the outside world. But I was trapped in a hotel, and the short trips to my friend Richard's computer barely gave me time to read email.

By the fifth day in Bangkok, the combination of emotions overwhelmed me. I used the demonic energy to write.

People could argue that CPU vision had left me unchanged since the same negative reactions came to haunt me that had haunted me before. Nevertheless, I had indeed changed. I now had awareness, and insights about them, and a deeper understanding of humanity and relationships.

Cyberspace is a new "realm of being" where emotional reactions stand out from their usual contexts.

I knew they were "my" mental monsters, existing apart from outer reality. They were as powerful as ever, but it was I who empowered them. The science of psychology has always noted that insight was the first step in therapy, from the psychoanalytic school to the Gestalt school:

Insight (psychoanalysis)
Awareness of the meaning and unconscious origin of one's behavior, symptoms, and the emotional processes which underlie them, this being a prerequisite to any therapeutic change.

Insight (Gestalt)
The main factor in learning characterized by grasping of those relationships leading to the solution of a problem, based on perceptual reorganization of previous experience. Once insight occurs it can promptly be repeated and applied to new situations. (Wolman, 1973)

The monsters were not all bad, either, since they created a tremendous source of energy. Energy and motivation can be muses. Where would I be without the

The first object of social analysis ought, I think, to be ordinary, actual behavior—its structure and its organization. However, the student, as well as his subjects, tends to take the framework of everyday life for granted; he remains unaware of what guides him and them. Comparative analysis of realms of being provides one way to disrupt this unselfconsciousness. Realms of being other than the ordinary provide natural experiments in which a property of ordinary activity is displayed or contrasted in a clarified and clarifying way. The design in accordance with which everyday experience is put together can be seen as a special variation on general themes, as ways of doing things that can be done in other ways. Seeing these differences (and similarities) means seeing. What is implicit and concealed can thus be unpacked, unraveled, revealed. (Goffman: 564) monsters? Unmotivated? Dull? Lazily at peace? As physical pain calls for relieving action, so do the monster/muses. They make me brave and heroic. They push me to excel, to differentiate and distinguish myself. Even though, thanks to insights I'd gained from CPU vision, I isolated them as illogical notions during that visit to Thailand, I couldn't bear their discomfort.

Writing by the pool in the Bangkok hotel wasn't enough. The monsters took control of my body, sending unnerving chemicals through my bloodstream. With the flood of them, I wanted to run run run. I knew I'd be taking the bad feelings with me, but changing the outer scenario has helped quell them in the past.

Hence, I did what I'd done eight years earlier when fraught with similar emotions—I fled to the island of Ko Samet.

To escape the sense of betrayal triggered by a Thai boyfriend, I'd spent seven months on Ko Samet where I learned to windsurf. Every time I lifted the sail and rode the seas, I told myself the enchantment of whisking with the wind was my reward for giving up the guy. Bliss instead of anguish. What a bargain! Those months on Ko Samet were heaven. I'd converted monster energy into muse energy without realizing what I was doing.

When planning the 1996 trip to Thailand, I didn't intend to return to Ko Samet, but when I couldn't stand Bangkok another second, I changed my airline ticket to allow me an extra week in Thailand and hopped on a bus for Ko Samet.

Immediately on arrival, I relaxed. I felt at peace and looked back in stupefaction at the intensity of the hellfire that had befallen me in Bangkok. How could I have been so crazy? But now I knew why I'd been so crazy.

As I spent an hour each day windsurfing—flying with the wind, my body remembering its mastery of balance—I knew that the demonic energy from an emotional response had brought me there. Next, I luxuriated as a temple-trained Thai woman massaged my muscles into ecstasy. I closed my eyes as her expert fingers kneaded my legs. I heard birds chirp and Japanese tourists jabber and small waves rolling to shore. From the restaurant of my bungalow lodge came Thai music, an exotic beat with bells. Nothing could have been better. The masseuse told me to turn over so she could attend to my back. I opened my eyes and caught a glimpse of rippling sea, shimmering palm trees, a striped bird pecking at a slice of discarded watermelon. No sight could have surpassed that one. The masseuse bent my arm backward in an invigorating stretch.

While her fingers worked my body I heard: *screech*, *screech*, *chirp chirp chirp*; a *drip-pause*, *drip-pause* of rain soaking through an awning from an earlier shower, the grumbling from the generator that electrified the lodge; the *brmm* of a speedboat. Nirvana.

I'd been in that exact Ko Samet heaven eight years earlier when I fled the misery of the Thai boyfriend whom I felt didn't appreciate me, didn't love me, didn't care about my feelings. The psychological pain of being with him equaled the pain of a broken bone. Was it a broken heart? I couldn't even glamorize it by calling it that. I didn't truly love the Thai with whom I shared few cultural experiences. The distress came not from a broken heart but from my insecurities, my frustrated wish to be cherished and adored—the same frustration I felt when a MOO man didn't return my affection, even though he'd never seen my picture, didn't know who I was, didn't know "me."

The Thai boyfriend told me "I love you," but monster emotions interpreted events and I heard: "I love this image I have of you and this arrangement we have where I gain status in my friends' eyes because I have an American girlfriend."

After the massage, I rented a water scooter. *"Pay con dio, mai?"* (You go alone?), the boat boy asked me.

"Pay con dio" (I go alone), I answered, unafraid to be far from shore. I knew the feeling of control I'd have racing over the water, bouncing across the wake of a passing ferry. I needed that feeling. Control and mastery are my nectars. They chase away the bugaboos. To kill a guest on the Palace or to hop over a wave on the sea brings the euphoria of power.

For dinner I ate squid in chili oil at a seaside restaurant in front of a TV showing a video about the Scottish rebellion against the English. The movie hero suffered the murder of his parents and the woman he loved, then he rose through his hurt to lead an uprising. From pain came motivation, from need for revenge came action.

Emotion evokes a response. A VR emotion is as real as an RL emotion. The distress I felt at the announcement of Dakota's wedding was the same as with the imagined rejection of my recent lover in Bangkok. Both situations involved circumstances unrelated to me, and to both I reacted in ways unconnected to the actual events.

As I lounged on a Ko Samet beach chair, I remembered

the words at the Bangkok conference I'd just participated in, on the management of therapeutic communities for drug addicts. A speaker emphasized the dynamics of the process where clients interacted with each other and examined their motives. "The evil I dimly perceive in myself, I try to stamp out in others."

Had that dynamic played itself out on me? Was I trying to stamp out a characteristic of myself and not of the other person? Who had cared less for their partner's soul—me or my Thai boyfriend? Me or my Western lover? Me or Dakota? Had I been fighting my own shadow?

On the other hand, there I was in paradise on Ko Samet. If the Bangkok reaction had been neurotic, than I'm blessed to have that particular neurosis. At that moment I loved being me.

A scruffy red mutt with matted tufts and leathery bald spots lived at my bungalow lodge. During the hot midday hours, he carved a spot for himself in the shade of an overturned canoe.

As I relaxed on the beach a Thai woman walked along the shoreline, carrying plastic bags denoting her return from a shopping trip. Behind her trotted an unleashed gray dog. The scruffy red pooch spotted the intruder and dashed into the sun. He struck a menacing pose an inch away from the other dog. The gray dog cowed as its owner walked on unaware. It hesitated then slunk slowly after the woman. The red dog growled and stiffened its muscles. The gray dog stopped, tail between its legs, crouching with a pleading look. Then he moved on at a crawl. Red made a threatening charge but backed off before touching the trespasser. He followed the gray dog until they reached the end of the lodge's land, where different-colored chairs marked the start of the next one.

Red stopped and the gray ran to catch up with the woman.

Territoriality! Red had assumed a territorial stance over the lodge. I identified with that feeling. That same monster resided in me. Red and I shared a common feeling, despite his scruffy fur and my strawberry-smelling shampooed hair. Was this psychological determinism?

I felt I had the same sense of territoriality as the red dog. I claim territory on a person, like I did with Jagwire, and if I sense an intruder, my defender instinct kicks in. I was no longer in MOO love with Jagwire when I spotted him with Zeden, yet I'd sent my asp to bite off his dick. I didn't want Zeden to touch it. I hadn't wanted Dakota, yet I felt my territory had been invaded when Robin announced her wedding to him.

How much are our minds and bodies like an organic computer terminal, preprogrammed with some templates of primitive origins, humanized by the species-specific development of Homo sapiens, and shaped by our early environment? And how much of our physical and emotional needs can be satisfied in cyberspace? I know that virtual realms can, indeed, fulfill some of these needs. Humans have animal urges, altered to fit our species. Cyberspace, by removing these desires from the physical plane, satisfies them in a wholly human medium, while exposing the primitive basis from which they stem.

What about our need to belong to a community? Can it be compared with a wolf's drive to belong to a pack?

Maybe we have a similar instinct, modified to suit our breed.

> We do seek community. There's no question about it. But also we're scared of it. So we seek a safe community, one in which we needn't be fully known. We want to preserve as much as we can of our privacy, our conveniences, as well as the freedom to pick up and move on. (Keyes, 1980:418-419)

Cyberspace would fit that perspective perfectly.

A centipede crawled along my beach table, its legs rising and falling in perfect synchronization, one behind the other. When it stopped, its legs continued to rise and fall but without propelling the insect forward. It looked like fifty people dancing a jig. My eyes feasted on the wonders of nature.

When I fled Bangkok the first time eight years earlier and landed on Ko Samet, eventually I found a new Thai boyfriend, named Toom. In 1996, I saw Toom's friend working in the same restaurant where they'd both been waiters when I met them. I heard news of Toom and the friend asked: "You want to telephone? I have Toom's number in Samut Prakaan."

I called him.

"I've been married and divorced twice," Toom told me. "Now I'm grown man, thirty years old. Before I was boy."

I had to think fast about how old I was supposed to be. Toom had been sixteen years younger than I, but I'd lied, saying I was only five years older. That would make me thirty-five now, not forty-six.

The 1996 Bangkok trip was confronting me with various sorts of realities—past lies, the passing of time, the inner coding of monsters, animal instincts. Reconnecting with Toom also made me realize how personal encounters affect people forever.

Toom had been a Ko Samet fling, a playful cross-cultural (and cross-generational) relationship, but I now realized he was a permanent part of my life's memories. Toom would be with me forever, just as I was part of him. Would The Necromancer remember me from all the time we spent together in the Patpong Bar on Sprawl MOO? I'm sure I'll always remember Rocker the Sprawl God and Jim Bumgardner the Palace creator. Both had inspired me with their ability to bring their ideas to life. And having Galactica as my best girlfriend when I'd met her in person as a male had opened me up to accepting people for who they were on alternative levels, allowing me to enjoy someone for specific aspects of themselves.

My time with Toom had been sweet. He'd triggered none of my unpleasant switches. On Ko Samet, I was a pampered leisure-class person. I wallowed in the luxury toys of the tourist. With my attentive Thai boyfriend, I hadn't a care in the world.

The only monster Toom invoked was obsession. My RL and VR obsessions are the same. Periodically during the seven months I had lived on the island, I returned to Bangkok to pick up mail. During those times I went bananas trying to call the island to speak to him, the radio link often being down. Like a madwoman I'd yell at the switchboard operator: "I MUST CALL KO SAMET!"

"No connection," she'd repeat, imploring me with her eyes not to accuse her.

"TRY AGAIN. VERY IMPORTANT," I'd demand, the words turning to shrieks as the hours passed.

The obsession monster with Toom was the same one that compelled me to do the @user command over and over on the MOO, searching for my love object, the person who momentarily occupied the love-object slot in my brain where the obsession monster lurked. When the slot was filled—by a faceless name on the computer, a furry avatar, a Thai boy—it sprang to life.

"You remember when we danced in the rain?" Toom asked me now.

"Yes! That was so great. After the disco!"

"I was thirsty and you went with me to get water."

That moment of spontaneous bliss was a high point in my life. Toom frequently woke in the middle of the night dying of thirst. It happened that night at two A.M. with pouring rain clattering on the roof. We knew nothing would be open except the disco at the end of the beach.

"Go," I told him, since his whining ensured I wouldn't get back to sleep till he quenched his thirst. But he didn't want to get wet so he stayed there moaning, "I'm so thirsty."

Obviously I'd get no rest with this problem. I dressed and pulled him out of bed and said, "I'm taking you for water."

"No, it's okay. Go back to bed. You don't have to *kreng chai.*" (be bothered). He protested, but I dragged him to his feet and pushed him out the door.

In seconds we were soaked but the hot air made it not unpleasant. We walked along the shore toward the bright lights of the disco, all other establishments in darkness. While Toom went to the bar for water the music caught me and I moved my hips and shoulders. The dancing enraptured me.

Thirst over, Toom joined me and we danced under the canopy with the other night owls.

"Okay, we go home now," he said. We danced down the steps back to the beach. Rain cascaded over us as if we were beneath a waterfall. Toom and I kicked our feet as we pranced in the surf and kissed, carousing in the downpour. We danced and twirled and fell laughing and hugging into the sea.

"You remember that night, too? So do I."

I told Toom I'd be back in Bangkok for only a day before having to fly home.

"I come see you," he said. "My office not far from your hotel."

I didn't want to meet him, preferring to go to Richard's house and play on his computer. I wanted to connect to my Internet family. Toom and I ended in an argument.

After hanging up, annoyed, I wondered if I wasn't the despicable person I always feared I'd find the other person to be. Was the evil I dimly perceived in myself what so scared me of other people?

Vacationers think of Ko Samet as a fantasy world, not a real one. Like going online, out of the touchable world of home and office, a vacation offers the same suspension of reality. Western men play with Thai prostitutes with the same nonchalance we play with our cyber lovers. I was shocked when Toom told me that Et, whom I remembered as a twelve-year-old boy, had died of a heroin overdose. When I'd first found Ko Samet, I noted the "Ko Samet Boys," perfect male specimens, and I loved seeing them with Western women. What a switch from Bangkok, where Western men drooled over Thai women. Through Toom and his friends, I empathized with the clash between the lives of the Thais locked into optionless poverty and the Westerners' rich lives full of opportunity. I'd joked how it felt good to be on the side that had the advantages. We Westerners could vacation in Thailand—in a fog of unreality—and then return home without considering the consequences of anything we'd done abroad.

One night at the café where Toom went after work, he introduced me to his Thai friend who'd just returned from Sweden. The friend had gone to visit his Western girlfriend whom he'd met on Ko Samet and who'd just given birth to their child. He'd sold all his possessions for the plane fare. But once there, the ex-girlfriend and her Swedish family refused to see him. The fantasy romance from the exotic resort didn't carry over into the reality of the woman's life in Sweden. He could find no job to support himself, so he returned to Ko Samet, depressed.

Twelve-year-old Et had been the son of the woman who rented windsurfing equipment. I saw him lugging sails every day. I knew he aspired to be like the young men of Ko Samet with blond girlfriends on their arms and gold chains around their necks, presents from the girlfriends. Hearing that Et was dead made me face the seriousness of the reality that vacationers considered unreal. Et had been caught in the contrast of rich Westerners and poor Thais. At the time I'd felt so good being with Toom, being a Westerner, living a carefree existence, that I hadn't fretted over our respective realities. Toom had been a heavy drinker, as were his friends. I suspected that the Ko Samet boys had a hard time comparing themselves with the happy-go-lucky Western travelers. Now, eight years later, I was in Thailand for a conference on drug abuse. I'd written a book about hippies—middle-class, educated Westerners—having fun on heroin in the Goa sun; I'd programmed a MOO bot so cybernauts could get virtually stoned on heroin; and Et was dead of a heroin overdose. The seriousness of reality collided with what had seemed unserious unreality.

Online interactions can be an avenue for exploring our emotional hardwiring. Cyberspace offers insights in a pure form, without the physical intervention of a person or place, without tactile stimulation. We see what triggers a chain of emotions linked to unrelated events. Like links on a Web page, a click on an inner hot spot transports us to another place, half a planet, or half a lifetime, away.

Seeing isolated reactions allows us to step back and view them from a different perspective. Perhaps we can laugh at what frightens us, hurts us to murderous rage, or haunts us from long-gone ghosts. I still take things personally when someone makes an innocent remark; I log right on to the worldview I had as a five-year-old. However, as I huff and flame, shut off the computer, and cry,

I'm aware that I've tapped into a chip in my brain that runs its own program, and I have no way to Control-C (cancel) out of it.

Though I stomp around my apartment in upset or run away from Bangkok in distress, I also appreciate that the energy derived from those feelings impels me to action. I appreciate that my misdirected thoughts can drive me to fanciful heights. The monsters are not my enemy. They can be turned into muses. And with awareness we can see our animal natures and the beauty of the human, including our sexuality. The net has the potential for making us better, more sympathetic, human beings.

In addition to personal introspection, cyberspace is instigating a sexual revolution. It gives us a place to grow to a freer sexual mental health as we surrender safely to arousal and passion. Though religious groups continue to repress sexuality with threats of hell for sinners, cyber sex does not involve naked bodies touching naked bodies and the dangers of sexually transmitted diseases and unwanted pregnancies. Only in the past few decades has the subject of masturbation been openly discussed as something we all engage in, and the belief that it causes blindness laughed at. Previously, and even in the present, women who were conditioned to deny their sexual needs discovered how to achieve release in the dark, in private, and probably with guilt. Now, in cyberspace, they still start with anonymity but among others. They can experiment with sexual expressions, and by changing genders, both males and females get a better view of what it's like to be the opposite sex.

Back to Virtual Reality

After two and a half years of MOOing, I thought I was too smart and savvy to fall into another net-sex obsession. I was wrong. My present VR lover totally consumes me. Throughout the day, I fantasize about what I can do with him when we are online at the same time. He's married, but I've changed my mind about staying away from married men online. But I still don't want to mix my VR lovers with RL meetings. I know that whatever I've dreamed up in my mind will never match the real person, live, in the flesh.

I don't want to know Calculus's RL identity and I don't want him to know mine. I love that we can be two made-up characters and play out our sexual fantasies; though thoughts of him do fill my RL waking moments, our MOO lives are based totally on sex.

On the other hand, I'm not positive whether or not online affairs can affect real lives. The outcome of this will be analyzed in the future. We have no way of predicting how this will work out ten years from now.

Bibliography

Albright, Julie M. and Tom Conron, "Online Love: Sex, Gender, and Relationships in Cyberspace," electronic document, http://wwwscf.usc.edu/~albright

Arieti, Silvano, ed., *American Handbook of Psychiatry*, 2nd edition, Basic Books, New York, 1974.

Barlow, John Perry, "Crime and Puzzlement: Desperados of the DataSphere," *Whole Earth Review*, Sausalito, CA, Fall 1990, 45-57.

Benedikt, Claire, "TinySex Is Safe Sex," *Passionate Living*, Nov. 1994.

Bieber, Irving, et al., *Homosexuality: A Psychoanalytic Study*, Basic Books, New York, 1962.

Borsook, Paulina, "The Memoirs of a Token: An Aging Berkeley Feminist Examines Wired," in Lynn Cherny and Elizabeth Reba Weise, eds., *Wired Women: Gender and New Realities in Cyberspace*, Seal Press, 1996,

Brown, Wilmette, "Money for Prostitutes Is Money for Black Women," from the organization Black Women for Wages for Housework, New York, Feb. 1977.

Bruckman, Amy S., "Gender Swapping on the Internet," electronic document, 1994, http://www.oise.on.ca/~jnolan/muds/about_muds/asb/gen.

Bumgardner, Jim, "Wizard Manual," electronic document, sent by email to new wizards.

Carlstead, Sara M, "net.love," electronic document, http://info.acm.org/crossroads/xrds1-4/netlove.html.

Carson, Robert C., *Interaction Concepts of Personality*, Aldine Publishing Company, Chicago, 1969.

Chapman, Sally, *Love Bytes*, St. Martins's Press, 1996.

Ciskowski, David and Claire Benedikt, *MUDs: Exploring Virtual Worlds on the Internet*, Macmillan Publishing, 1995.

Clark, M. S., "Moods and Memory: Some Issues for Social and Personality Psychologists to Consider," in D. Kuiken, ed., *Mood and Memory: Theory Research and Applications*, Newbury Park, CA, Sage, 1991, 1-21.

Cohen, Eric., "Lovelorn Farangs: the Correspondence Between Foreign Men and Thai Girls," *Anthropological Quarterly* 59 (3), 114-127: 1986.

————,"Sensuality and Venality in Bangkok: The Dynamics of Cross-Cultural Mapping of Prostitution," *Deviant Behavior* 8, 223-234: 1987.

Curtis, Pavel, "Mudding: Social Phenomena in Text-Based Virtual Realities," electronic document, http://www.oise.on.ca/-jnolan/muds/about_muds/pavel.html.

de Sade, Marquis, *Justine* (1791), Grove Press, New York, 1965.

Dibbell, Julian, "Rape in Cyberspace," *The Village Voice*, Dec. 23, 1993.

————, "The Prisoner: Phiber Optik Goes Directly to Jail," *The Village Voice*, Jan. 12, 1994.

Ellis, H. C., & P. W. Asbrook, "The 'State' of Mood and Memory Research: A Selective Review," in D. Kuiken, ed., *Mood and Memory; Theory Research and Applications* Newbury Park, CA, Sage, 1991; 1-21.

Epstein, Samuel Latt, WOO Transaction Protocol (WTP) Copyright 1994, Picosof Systems, electronic document, http://sensemedia.net/woo.

Fischer, Claude S., *America Calling: A Social History of the Telephone to 1940*, University of California Press, Los Angeles, 1992.

Gebhard, Paul H., "Fetishism and Sadomasochism" in Martin S. Weinberg, ed., *Sex Research: Studies from the Kinsey Institute*, Oxford University Press, New York, 1976.

Gibson, William, *Neuromancer*, Ace Books, New York, 1984.

Goffman, Erving, *Frame Analysis: An Essay on the Organization of Experience*, Harvard University Press, Cambridge, 1974.

Holland, Norman N., "The Internet Regression," Electronic document, June 1996, http://www.slm-net.com/signum.htm.

Hudson, James A., "Four Girls in Stereo and Two Girls in Person Tell It All the Way It Is," in *Sir!* magazine, Jan. 1970.

Hymes, Dell, *Foundations in Sociolinguistics: An Ethnographic Approach*, University of Pennsylvania Press, Philadelphia: 1974.

Keyes, Ralph, "We, the Lonely People" in Joseph Hartog, J. Ralph Audy and Yehudi A. Cohen, eds., *The Anatomy of Loneliness*, International Universities Press, New York, 1980.

King, Storm A., "Effects of Mood States on Social Judgments in Cyberspace: Self Focused Sad People As the Source of Flame Wars," electronic document, 1996, http://www.coil.com/-grohol/storm1.html.

Kinsey, Alfred C., Wardell B. Pomeroy, and Clyde E. Martin, *Sexual Behavior in the Human Male*, W. B. Sanders Company, Philadelphia, 1948.

Kinsey, Alfred C., Wardell B. Pomeroy, Clyde E. Martin, and Paul H.Gebbard, *Sexual Behavior in the Human Female*, W. B. Sanders Company, Philadelphia, 1953.

Labov, William, *Sociolinguistic Patterns*, University of Pennsylvania, Philadelphia, 1984.

Leibowitz, Leila, "Perspective on the Evolution of Sex Differences," in Rayna R. Reiter, ed., *Toward an Anthropology of Women*, Monthly Review Press, New York, 1975.

Lodge, Dave (aka Corwin/Dworkin), "The Saga of WorldMOO: It Was the Best of MOOs; It Was the Worst of MOOs," electronic document, 1995.

Lorenz, Konrad, *King Solomon's Ring*, Crowell, New York, 1952.

Odzer, Cleo, *Patpong Sisters: An American Woman's View of the Bangkok Sex World*, Blue Moon-Arcade Books, New York, 1994.

———, *Goa Freaks: My Hippie Years in India*, Blue Moon Books, New York: 1995.

O'Neill, Molly, "The Lure and Addiction of Life On Line," *The New York Times*, Wednesday, Mar. 8, 1995, C1.

Ong, Achwa, "Industrialization and Prostitution in Southeast Asia," *Southeast Asia Chronicle*, Jan. 1985, p. 96.

Paroite, Somsak, "Virtual Sleaze in Cyberspace," *Nation*, a Thai newspaper, Bangkok, Nov. 1995.

Pearl, Mike and Christopher Francescani, "Cyber-Sex Suspect Accused by Two Others," *New York Post*, Dec. 9th, 1996, 4.

Quan, Tracy, "Talk of the Stroll," *Adam* 39:(9), Mar. 1995, 35.

Reid, Elizabeth M., "Electropolis: Communication and Community on Internet Relay Chat," Honors Thesis, University of Melbourne Dept. of History, 1991.

———, "Cultural Formations in Text-Based Virtual Realities," a thesis submitted in fulfillment of the requirements for the degree of Master of Arts, University of Melbourne, 1994.

Rheingold, Howard, *The Virtual Community: Homesteading on the Electronic Frontier*, Harper Perennial, New York, 1993.

Rosenberg, Michael S., "Virtual Reality: Reflections of Life, Dreams, and Technology: An Ethnography of a Computer Society," electronic document, 1992, http://www.oise.on.ca/-jnolan/muds/about_muds/ethnography.txt.

Schalbruch, Martin, "The Hind Legs of the Elephant," *Bangkok Post*, newspaper, Aug. 14, 1988, 25.

Sholton, Margaret, A. *Computer Addiction? A Study of Computer Dependency*, Taylor Francis, London, England, 1989.

Slatalla, Michelle and Joshua Quittner, *Masters of Deception: The Gang That Ruled Cyberspace*, HarperCollins, New York, 1995.

Stephenson, Neal, *Snow Crash*, Bantam Books, New York, 1992.

Suler, John, "Cyberspace as Psychological Space," electronic document, May 1996, http://www1.rider.edu/-suler/psycyber/psychspace.html.

————, "Computer and Cyberspace Addiction," electronic document, Aug. 1996, http://www1.rider.edu/-suler/psycyber/cybaddict.html.

————, "On Being a God: An Interview with Jim Bumgardner," electronic document, June 1996, http://www1.rider.edu/-suler/psycyber/jbum.html.

Sullivan, H. S., *The Interpersonal Theory of Psychiatry*, W. W. Norton, New York, 1953.

Tannahill, Reay, *Sex in History*, Scarborough House, USA, 1992.

Tisdale, Sally, *Talk Dirty to Me: An Intimate Philosophy of Sex*, Anchor Books, New York, 1995.

Wolman, Benjamin B. ed., *Dictionary of Behavioral Science*, Van Nostrand Reinhold Company, New York, 1973.

yduJ (a Lambda-MOO character), "yduJ's MOO Programmer's Tutorial," electronic document from Lambda MOO.

Cleo Odzer earned her Ph.D. in anthropology in 1990. Her dissertation on prostitution in Thailand was the basis for her first book, *Patpong Sisters: An American Woman's View of the Bangkok Sex World*. Her second book was *Goa Freaks: My Hippie Years in India*. She's had a public access TV show called *Cleo's Adventures* for two and a half years on Manhattan Neighborhood Network.